CROSSCURRENTS
PURSUING SOCIAL JUSTICE AND INTERRELIGIOUS WORK
SINCE 1950

CrossCurrents (ISSN 0011-1953; online ISSN 1939-3881) connects the wisdom of the heart with the life of the mind and the experiences of the body. The journal is operated through its parent organization, the Association for Public Religion and Intellectual Life (APRIL), an interreligious network of academics, activists, artists, and community leaders seeking to engage the many ways religion meets the public. Contributions to the journal exist at the nexus of religion, education, the arts, and social justice. The journal is published quarterly on behalf of the Association for Public Religion and Intellectual Life by the University of North Carolina Press.

The Association for Public Religion and Intellectual Life (formerly ARIL) is a global network of leaders, scholars, and social change agents who explore religious life, engage in intellectual inquiry, and lead ethical action in the world today. Their primary objective, especially through annual summer colloquia and *CrossCurrents*, is to bring together leading voices of our time to advocate for justice and to examine global spiritual and interreligious currents in both historical and contemporary perspectives.

A membership to APRIL includes access to *CrossCurrents* starting with Volume 58, 2008, though our partners at Project MUSE, monthly newsletters, early access to summer colloquium themes, a 40% on UNC Press books, and more. For more information, including membership and subscription rates, visit www.aprilonline.org.

This reissue of *CrossCurrents* was one of four issues published in 2012 as part of Volume 62. For a current masthead visit www.aprilonline.org.

© 2012 Association for Public Religion and Intellectual Life. All rights reserved.

ISBN 978-1-4696-6702-7 (Print)

CROSSCURRENTS

VOLUME 62, NO 1 ISSN 0011-1953

A SYMPOSIUM ON JEWISH LITURGY

4
Note About This Issue
Charles P. Henderson

5
Introduction
Vanessa L. Ochs

11
A Heart of Flesh: Beyond "Creative Liturgy"
Catherine Madsen

21
Response to Catherine Madsen
Randi Rashkover

29
Response to Catherina Madsen—God as Criterion of Jewish Liturgy
Steven Kepnes

33
Response to Catherine Madsen, "A Heart of Flesh: Beyond 'Creative Liturgy'"
Leah Hochman

37
Response to Catherine Madsen's Paper, "A Heart of Flesh: Beyond 'Creative Liturgy'"
Caroline Rody

40
Catherine Madsen Responds
Catherine Madsen

43
Law as Lyric, Lyric as Star Trek: A Reading of Kol Nidre
Eric Murphy Selinger

50
Kaplan's Approach to Prayer Appreciated and Challenged
Eric Caplan

61
On Poetry and Prayer
Rachel Barenblat

71
Poetry and Prayer
Edward Feld

75
Human Rights Need a Human Tradition
Gabriel Moran

89
*Theology After Obama—What Does Race Have to Do With It?:
A Racial Prolegomenon to American Theological Production
in the Twenty-first Century*
James W. Perkinson

110
*What Kind of Country?:
Economic Crisis, the Obama Presidency, the Politics of Loathing,
and the Common Good*
Gary Dorrien

143
Book Reviews

150
Notes on Contributors

CROSSCURRENTS
NOTE ABOUT THIS ISSUE

This issue of *CrossCurrents* falls into two parts. The first part, on the topic, "Jewish Liturgy," consists of a paper delivered by Catherine Madsen at a recent conference on Jewish Renaissances at the University of Virginia. The transcript of her presentation is followed by a series of responses by people who will be familiar to our readers. Reading this set of articles as a Christian, I see a number of parallels, if not a total match, with the similar, often agonizing struggle over "creative liturgy" within many Christian denominations. Such conversations have echoed in the sanctuaries and board rooms of congregations and denominational offices around the world for several decades and continue to do so today. And there are few topics more important for Christians, as well as Jews, to be engaged in. For liturgy lies at the heart and center of who we are as peoples, not only shaping our identity, but informing the ways in which we relate to each other within our diverse communities, as well as with the various publics we encounter every day.

The second part of this issue flows seamlessly from the first, moving out from the context of the sanctuary toward the broader civil society, and to the realm of politics in particular. Here we venture out from the more personal and subjective realm of the poet, toward those more public, contentious struggles over race, class, and how we negotiate our differences to become a people. Finally, Gary Dorrien sets the stage for the 2012 presidential election with his sweeping analysis of the Obama administration and its critics. By no means an apology for the often disappointing policies and decisions of this president's first term, Dorrien instead frames a positive agenda for a second Obama administration, one which could, quite possibly, move us forward, absent the constraints associated with anxiety about the likelihood of reelection.

Charles P. Henderson

CROSSCURRENTS

INTRODUCTION

Vanessa L. Ochs

The essays you are about to read are responses to Catherine Madsen's provocative and ongoing critique of new liturgy and her implicit challenges to liturgical creators to achieve excellence. Madsen shared her most recent thoughts in the context of a conference on Jewish Renaissances, held at the University of Virginia, on the occasion of the tenth anniversary of the UVA Jewish Studies program. A theological response was offered by Randi Rashover (George Mason University) and a literary response by Caroline Rody (University of Virginia). The conversation continues on, drawing to it the essays by Steven Kepnis (Colgate University) and Leah Hochman (Hebrew Union College—Jewish Institute of Religion/Los Angeles) that you will see here as well.

A conversation such as this is situated in the broader context of discussions of new religious ritual. (For this discussion, I propose that we use the term "ritual" most capaciously, so that it could include simple or elaborate ceremonies; objects; or the written words, music, and gestures of liturgies.) What might it mean to assess a new ritual that has been innovated in our lifetimes?

There is the matter of timing. It takes time for a new ritual to fully take shape and time too for people to overcome their anxieties about innovation. The kinks have to been ironed out, and the new ritual has to have already been able to gather about itself some of the patina of "authenticity" that familiarity deposits. When is it appropriate to step back and say, "OK, so what do we think?"

INTRODUCTION

There is the matter of who is empowered to stand in the place of judgment, or whose opinions "count." Everyday people who vote "with their feet?" Local clergy, denominational leaders, or the publication committees of the manuals that clergy draw upon? And what about the perspective of scholars of ritual, perhaps members of religious communities who are living with, even initiating, the innovations?

Imagine for a moment that such preliminary issues have been sufficiently resolved or set aside for the purpose of discussion, and only one question remains: *How* should a new ritual be evaluated? I will inquire about Jewish rituals and offer examples from Judaism, but I suspect that my line of inquiry might easily apply to other traditions.

It is a commonplace that many new Jewish rituals, ceremonies, liturgies, and ritual objects have been incubated in our own era and have flourished. There is ritual innovation occasioned by feminism, the Holocaust, and the birth of the State of Israel. There is innovation that responds to absences, marks the unmarked, shapes new collective memories, and reflects political and social changes. What is particularly distinctive about our era is the role of technology: thanks to the mimeograph machine, the copier, the fax, the Internet, and social networking platforms, new Jewish rituals "go viral." On the eve of September 11, 2001, Jewish communities throughout America seeking to hold vigils were downloading a service of traditional prayers and selected poems, and even a prayer immediately composed Jeffrey A. Spitzer. As we can see from one of its verses that I cite here, it placed the destruction of the day in relationship to the classic site of destruction, that of Jerusalem, creating a liturgical apparatus for creating meaning at a time of shock:

> New York and Washington, shining cities,
> Diminished like Jerusalem after the destruction of the holy Temple,
> need Your comfort, and our aid;
> help us to maintain our courage and our efforts to support our people.[1]

Historically, we know that Jews have always been busy innovating ritual, either because of crisis, exile, trauma or, in gentler times, the necessities of accommodating to changing cultural contexts, and novel ideas. The impulse to evaluate a ritual, by critiquing both practical and spiritual implications, is familiar too. The Babylonian Talmud preserves one of my favorite examples of a "best practices" discussion that takes place across generations. In debate form, it evaluates how travelers who are riding on a donkey should go about saying the thrice-daily *Shmoneh Esrei* prayer, said while standing. It is also referred to as the *Amidah*, "the standing"—obviously, the standing part is important. The Mishna states that if you are traveling by donkey, you should dismount and pray. But the Talmud offers variations: if you are riding on a donkey and it is time to pray and it just so happens that someone can hold your donkey, then by all means, dismount and pray. And if you are alone? Sit on your donkey and pray. But the most conclusive voice, the one that rules the day even as it introduces what seems like a transgressive practice, says that you should stay seated on your donkey and pray the standing prayer whether you have a donkey-minder or not. Given that a traveler's mind is unsettled with worries about making time (and about the donkey running off), it is already hard enough to stay focused enough for meaningful prayer. Bottom line; the new ritual of remaining seated on your donkey if you are traveling, and saying the "standing" prayer is not only acceptable, but preferable. This classical model demonstrates how debaters insert criteria that they believe are appropriate. In this case, there is respect for God, respect for the accepted prayer practices of the day, and concern about the capacity of the one who engages in the ritual to have *kavvanah*, spiritual engagement. In this case, sages (who had apparently gone on their share of donkey rides) decided spiritual engagement mattered most.

What are some of the criteria brought into play when deliberating over new ritual in our time? Now, as in the past, permissibility matters. Some will evaluate the new ritual in terms of their understanding of *halachah*, Jewish law. Is this new ritual in accordance with *halachah*, is it obviously a transgression, or is the matter so difficult to resolve that only many sages, in conference with each other, can arrive at some decision after what can be protracted debate, as it has been in the case of same-sex marriage ceremonies. Jews who use other criteria for making religious decisions (such as the power of tradition, the history of the community, or the demands of ethics) will come up with other standards that guide them. The problem with permissibility is always this: Who is making the judgment and how? Moreover, matters of permissibility inevitably create a debate between those whom I have termed guardians of continuity and agents of change. Simply put, the guardians of continuity tend to honor the traditions of the past and often feel that any innovations will erode precious inheritances of the past. Agents of change tend to believe that tradition is kept vibrant only when it flexibly and respectfully adapt to new situations.[2] Endurance is another criteria evaluating how new ritual has withstood the test of time. The ceremony for welcoming baby girls into the covenantal community, practiced in various forms for over forty years, is a good example of a ritual that has been around long enough so that people now speak of it as "the traditional" ceremony for baby girls. (A text for it can be found in the rabbinic manuals of various denominations, another indication of endurance.) But "shelf life" is not always the relevant measure for new ritual. For instance, providing a fifth cup of wine at one's Passover seder and offering readings that addressed the need to free Soviet Jewry constituted an excellent, effective ritual in its time. But that prayer has already been "answered," so to speak, and the broader Jewish community has decided that it is no longer a touchstone for community engagement.[3]

Popularity is another criterion. Has the new ritual attracted "buy-in" from a broad number of constituents, allowing improvisation in different setting and situations? Holocaust memorial services, while their form has not quite coalesced, would be an example. But a customer-based assessment can be problematic. For instance, it is clear that more Jews practice ethnic "kosher-style eating" (not mixing milk and meat together, not eating shellfish or pork) than strict kashrut, the traditional dietary laws. Is the popular and more doable practice "superior"? That would be a complicated debate, one that would call for some distinction between ethnic/cultural behaviors and religious ones.

And how about evaluating a new ritual by its efficacy? Does the innovation do the work it promises, perhaps touching more people and more deeply than a traditional form? Many would claim that folk-inflected *"Mi Sheberach"* healing prayer composed by Debbie Friedman, of blessed memory, has the power to persuade people that they are not alone when they are ill, God is present, the Jewish community is present, and their suffering is diminished. And now the flip side: what about those whose understanding about structure of the worship service and the ways in which personal requests are linked to Torah honor does not allow them to experience connection to tradition, community and God when the medium is a folk song blending Hebrew and English?

I could offer many more criteria: does the new ritual fills a pressing need, does it address a crisis, does it recognize changes in the community's composition I, myself (full disclosure, as journalists say: I am one of those academic scholars of new ritual who also plays various roles in innovating Jewish rituals) tend to evaluate new rituals according to three criteria. First, does it link to the classic texts or text structures, such as Talmudic conversation, the structure of liturgies, or legal writs? Second, does it make an overt or symbolic connection to traditional ritual objects (as Miriam's cup is linked to that of Elijah) or actions (as lighting six candles in memory of the Jewish who perished in the Holocaust is linked to the lighting of memorial candles)? And third, does it reflect core Jewish understandings (such as the one God, the place of ancestors, and the obligation to lead a sanctified life) and keep faith with them?

That said, there is no absolute set of criteria that would be absolutely relevant in each scenario or community. It is exceedingly hard to evaluate the new rituals we are in the process of living with and tweaking, especially when they bring with them challenging new paradigms for thinking about what it means to live in holiness. Making it harder still is our awareness, made most clear by Rabbi Lawrence Hoffman in "Beyond the Text," that ritual forms are not just templates for objects or scripts: they are enacted, experienced, and manipulated in specific contexts and can have great or little meaning depending upon the community one is in, the mood that has been established, and the affective shifts between the fixed and the inspired.

But innovation, at the very least because it challenges and disrupts the familiar, demands some kind of response other than, "Oh no!" or "Whatever..." Catherine Madsen initiates the inquiry, positing a very particular set of demanding standards as she compares the newest liturgies to those that have been received and embraced.

Vanessa Ochs teaches in the Department of Religious Studies and the Program in Jewish Studies at the University of Virginia. She is the author of Inventing Jewish Ritual.

Notes

1. http://www.jewishfederations.org/page.aspx?id=2381, accessed on January 26, 2011.
2. See Ochs Vanessa, 2007, *Inventing Jewish Ritual*, Philadelphia: Jewish Publication Society, pp. 159–62.
3. I suspect that if there were large communities of religious Jews from the former Soviet Union, then their plight and subsequent rescue might continue to be addressed in the Passover Haggadah.

A HEART OF FLESH
Beyond "Creative Liturgy"
Catherine Madsen

In the mid-1980s, a young acting student, Thomas Richards, took a two-week workshop in California with the great Polish director Jerzy Grotowski. Grotowski was the intellectual heir of Konstantin Stanislavski and the founder of laboratory theater, a school of acting based on intensive improvisation and concentrated emotional power. His aim was to create what he called "a poor theatre," in which the actor's sharply honed skills took the place of elaborate sets and props. Sometimes he spoke of a "holy theatre," whose spareness and intensity could raise performance to the level of ritual. As a first assignment in the workshop, Grotowski asked Richards and the other students to show him what they thought they would be doing there. They put together a short piece that involved spontaneous singing, chanting, dancing, and running barefoot into the prickly desert. To their confusion, Grotowski denounced these initial attempts as "universal human banalities" (20) and sent three of them off to renew their tetanus shots.

For the first solo assignment, each student was to compose a brief "mystery play" built on a traditional song from childhood. Richards put together a sequence of symbolic actions to express his feelings for his father, added some unrehearsed elements at the last minute, and gave a performance he felt as cathartic, soul-baring and exhausting. Grotowski watched him impassively and said simply, "Please repeat."

As Richards discovered over the next two weeks through much humiliating critique, Grotowski's use of improvisation was not at all free-form and spontaneous. It was highly structured and painstakingly revised. It ruthlessly cannibalized past experience and spontaneous emotion for clear and repeatable moves. Richards had assumed that emotional intensity would communicate itself simply by being intense; as it turned out, his audience only saw him working himself into a frenzy for no intelligible reason. Long afterward—by this time having worked as Grotowski's assistant for several years—Richards reflected, "I had mistaken agitated nerves for true emotions; I had avoided true practical work, and tried to pump an emotional state" (36).

Anyone familiar with contemporary liberal Jewish liturgy will recognize some of the same beginners' mistakes. The quick and uncritical construction, the emphasis on kavvanah or "intention," the assumption that feeling conveys itself automatically, the effort to generate ecstatic states without first having laid a solid structural groundwork: these are more or less the working methods of the Jewish Renewal movement, feminist experimental liturgy, the current Reconstructionist siddur, and (minus the ecstatic states) liberal Jewish interpretive prayer generally. The emphasis is on "having a liturgical experience," not on "performing a liturgical act," and the Orthodox sense of fulfilling a liturgical obligation is out of the picture. Yet an experience is not always available for the asking. Even kavvanah cannot be reliably summoned, and is apt to evaporate at the fatal imperative, "Please repeat."

Liturgy differs from theater in several obvious ways. It is meant for participants, not for spectators; it is slower-moving and less compactly dramatic; it is in no sense an entertainment but makes a direct, naked effort to intervene in our lives. Theater, like literature generally, operates at one remove from actually giving commands. In this sense, liturgy is not and cannot be a purely literary form. But liturgy shares with theater the need for aesthetic and psychological coherence. The participant in liturgy, like the audience at a play, must have the sense of being expertly guided. Inept writing, sudden gratuitous political gestures, and a sweet tooth for novelty—those hallmarks of contemporary "creative liturgy"—produce neither holy theater nor durable prayer. The leopards in Kafka's parable break into the temple so dependably that they finally become part of the ritual, but there are kavvanot that will never be more than irritants no matter how often we hear them.

On what basis can "creative liturgy" be evaluated? Does it want to be evaluated? It turns away critique with those two dread adjectives, *elitist* and *judgmental*. But repetition leads inevitably to evaluation. A one-time audience may not be highly critical of the play, but the actors who must produce the same effects night after night know when something works badly. The first-time bar mitzvah guest may enjoy the stray Mary Oliver poem for its vividness and theological neutrality, but if the poem is used every week, the regular participants will soon find it a detour from the real work. Even more of a detour are the poems of non-poets, usually rabbis, printed in prayer books for use *ad infinitum* by their colleagues: the rabbis may be admirable teachers, counselors, and administrators, but their poems are exhausted by the first use. Certain Buddhist-influenced rabbis dismiss language as mere spiritual white noise, a stance incongruous in a religion of the Book and a handy excuse for not revising their poems. The first draft with one or two promising phrases gives way, not to a concentrated and compelling final draft but to a new first draft on another subject with one or two more promising phrases. Grotowski excoriated this approach in his acting students as "tourism." In liturgical circles, rather as in grade school, the word "creativity" is not an incitement to artistic concentration but a code for dilettantism, a messy, happy splashing in raw materials with no sense of the long term. The mere suggestion of the long term provokes the intellectual equivalent of the reproachful stare and the trembling lower lip.

Given the example of the traditional liturgy, including the Psalms, why do contemporary liturgists aim so low? Why are they willing to present so unconvincingly the social and theological principles they are convinced of? Why do they all but explicitly renounce aesthetic competence? The recent book *Ritual and Its Consequences: The Limits of Sincerity*, by Adam Seligman, Robert Weller, Michael Puett, and Bennett Simon, gives a cogent analysis of the situation. The authors make the case that contemporary liturgical culture values sincere expression of feeling and belief far above the imaginative or "subjunctive" mode of traditional ritual. "Sincerity," in this sense, repudiates any statement or emotion dissonant with the modern sensibility; far from trying to equal the past, we are meant to reject its formulas as benighted and irrelevant and construct acceptable substitutes in a hurry. The subjunctive mode, by contrast, is not quite about us; it does not reveal its relevance all at once but yields it gradually through participation. Sincerity is concerned with the "as-is"—reinforcing our present collective self-concept—and the subjunctive with the "as-if," a reality we bring into being through collective ritual practice. Seligman et al. suggest that religious ritual, like social ritual, is meant to function more or less as a reflex; it is not meant to be consciously assented to each time but to be performed automatically. Just as in social ritual we say "please" and "thank you" whether we mean it or not, in religious ritual we address and appeal to a God we may or may not believe in, regardless of our private commitment to the speech act. The authors say that

> In doing a ritual, the whole issue of our internal states is irrelevant. What you *are* is what you are *in the doing*, which is of course an external act. This is very different from modernist concerns with sincerity and authenticity….Getting it *right* is not a matter of making outer acts conform to inner beliefs. Getting it right is doing it again and again and again—it is an act of world construction. (24)

Paradoxically, sincerity is a constantly receding goal: it disappears from the hastily codified new formulas as soon as our attitudes change, or as soon as we expect our children to share them. The subjunctive mode, not being based on belief, is actually broadly inclusive, whereas sincerity, which believes in inclusion, tends toward the inquisitorial. For sincerity, say Seligman et al., "there is never enough evidence, cannot be, anywhere, at any time." Even the Mary Oliver poem or the quasi-Buddhist dismissal of words comes to function as a boundary enforcer, a loyalty oath. As a result, the traditional forms are forced away from the subjunctive and become charged with a counter-sincerity that turns them into loyalty oaths in their turn. Fundamentalist religion, as Seligman and his colleagues remind us, is quintessentially modern and savagely sincere: it retaliates against the disruptions of modernist protest by recreating them in full force from the opposing side. The totalistic nature of sincerity, whether on the right or the left, profoundly threatens the slow, patient courtesy of liturgical world construction. Sincerity specializes in pumping emotion; it intercepts and re-routes—to the right or to the left—the loyalty that in ritual practice belongs only to God.

Stanislavski once said, "Don't talk to me about feeling. We cannot set feeling. We can only set physical action" (Richards 67). He came to this idea late in his career and did not live to develop it; it was Grotowski who carried it further. As the young Thomas Richards gradually found, "setting physical action" meant conveying emotion not by reproducing it *psychically* at every performance but by attentively searching for the *physical* and vocal markers of the emotion, breaking them down into small enough units to engage the actor's attention at every performance, and rigorously rehearsing the whole series of units until it was fluent and compelling. Essentially, it was the artistic equivalent of scientific method: the search for the reproducible result. Richards broke through to understanding several months later while carrying an object to someone during a group exercise. Grotowski suddenly stopped him and said, "Yes, something is there....You were walking for someone." Richards had been remembering a childhood incident of bringing a present to his father in the hospital, defying the nurses who said he was too young to be there alone. Grotowski did not know what the memory was, but he saw its signature. "Every time...I was to remember how I had walked for my father in the hospital. I should not remember my feeling, but the way in which I had done it, and for whom....I should *not try to feel* proud. That I cannot do, but I can ask myself: *in that moment when I was proud, how did I walk?*" (66-67).

Da lifnei mi atah omed, "know before whom you stand." This injunction, written over the ark in many synagogues, is a prompt or trigger for this kind of physical memory. It does not tell you that you stand before Freud or Marx or Mordecai Kaplan, before Betty Friedan or Judith Plaskow, before Eric Voegelin or the Satmar Rebbe or Sarah Palin; it does not tell you in so many words that you stand before God. It asks you to discover—the verb *da* is the one used for carnal knowledge—through intimate experience to whom you hold yourself responsible. This is not the search for rational assent or ecstatic trance or even personal authenticity; it is the search for emotional and moral landmarks. To ask yourself before whom you stand—or "For whom did I walk?"—is to discover the *private* loyalty, which is inviolable and stands against the shallow public allegiance. The formulaic sincerities of left and right ask you to be loyal to feminist theory or free enterprise or the 1960s. The private loyalty forces all this through the narrow channel of your experience, where generalities drop away. At the heart of our subjectivity we discover something uncompromising: not what we want to *express* but what we want to be *held to* brought back to from every distraction. This is where reproducible results begin.

If we're going to talk about a Jewish renaissance, we should be clear what we're asking for. A renaissance is not just a burst of enthusiasm or a proliferation of theory: it is an exuberant and disciplined pursuit of high competence that involves a whole culture. Renaissance work is exacting and accurate; it is interested in measurement, pattern, proportion, fine detail and mental acuity. Its striking emotional effects are achieved through strict observation and full control of one's medium. Renaissance artists are intensely interested in tradition, not because tradition is already perfect and finished, but because tradition serves as a scaffolding for a new attempt at perfection. The sense of rebirth is the sense of *mastery*, potency, competence to achieve: the sense of having the tools, techniques, and energies to produce exceptional work.

Every art, not only the actor's, is accomplished through a series of small reproducible units. A visual artist establishes critical points and rough lines, refines the sketchy lines into shapes and accurate contours, and then represents the play of light on the object through variations in line quality and subtly graded shadow shapes. A musician learns the notes of a piece and, by playing them hundreds of times, learns to play them each time as if discovering them for the first time. A singer makes constant fine adjustments of posture, breath, vocal placement, pronunciation, projection, expressiveness and remoteness. A poet listens for intersections of sound and rhythm and meaning, fixing emotion so the words must yield it at each reading, forcing words to function as physical actions. The supposed opposition between sincerity and tradition, spontaneity and repetition, is artificial: you need the repetition to render the spontaneity. "The...tension between the inner process and the form strengthens both," wrote Grotowski. "The form is like a baited trap, to which the spiritual process responds spontaneously and against which it struggles" (*Towards a Poor Theatre* 17).

A specifically Jewish renaissance, presumably, stands on Torah, avodah, and gemilut chasadim—study, worship, and acts of kindness: a sort of three-point perspective for evaluating one's work. It's comparatively easy to evaluate Torah and gemilut chasadim: we can measure a person's knowledge of texts, accuracy with Torah trope, and indebtedness to Jewish modes of thought. We can see the consequences of acts of kindness: see individuals and institutions flourishing, count the money given in tzedakah and read the donor plaques. But in avodah, no longer measured as it was in the Temple, in he-goats and bullocks and yearling lambs, but in "the service of the heart," how do we recognize exceptional work? In liberal Jewish liturgy, where exceptional work is not even the aim, what would a renaissance look like?

In traditional Judaism, the structure of small reproducible units is the system of mitzvot. Some of these are specifically liturgical and some are not, but all that still obtain in the absence of the Temple are practiced regardless of kavvanah or willingness. It makes no difference how you feel about observing Shabbat, davvening three times a day, keeping kosher, or giving money to the poor, you do it because you are commanded. In non-halachic Judaism, which from its inception has been defined by the practices it does not require, what is the structure of small reproducible units? The guidelines for "inclusive language" do not demand or generate a high level of skill. The new prayers are still at the level of running barefoot into the desert, the work of people who do not understand their craft. Is there, even latently, another structure in liberal Judaism that will serve?

In the absence of halacha, what remains is biblical text—shorn of its authority to establish communal norms, but retaining and even exerting more strongly its literary authority. The Bible is actually more disturbing when the talmudic fence is knocked down: there is no layer of mild, pacific commentary between us and the trickster patriarchs and matriarchs, the corrosive relations of Moses and the Israelites, the prophetic threats and promises relaying the wrath and love of an uncanny God. If liberal Jews were hoping to look more like Protestants, they got more than they bargained for in this confrontation with the raw biblical text. Understandably, some of them today would rather have Mary Oliver poems about nature or quasi-Buddhist reassurances that words are mere chatter. The Bible's demand for sincerity is embedded in wounding language, which cannot be appeased by theological or theoretical or ritual adjustments but only by physical actions. God's commands, whether we take them to mean the system of mitzvot or something more ambiguous, are meant to yield a reproducible result: deeds, *ma'asey yadeinu*, the work of our hands.

If liberal Judaism has a function other than relaxing the standards of observance, it might be to create a new standard of attention: to discover what Jeremiah meant when he said that in place of the covenant we broke, God would put his Torah in our inward parts and write it on our hearts (31:32). "And they shall teach no more every man his neighbor and every man his brother, saying, Know the Lord: for they shall all know me, from the least unto the greatest of them" (31:33). Is this a statement of spiritual democracy or of an unremitting imaginative demand? Protagoras' maxim "Man the measure of all things" was understood in his own time as a statement of subjectivity, even relativism: you may feel the cold more or less than I do, you may like Mary Oliver and I may like Jeremiah, and how can either of us be wrong? But in the Renaissance it was differently understood: the human mind is a measuring instrument. We calculate and calibrate, revise and rework; we are in the grip of a difficult task.

If a renaissance involves reworking—or cannibalizing—classical material and techniques for the use of a later time with its own preoccupations, the Bible is not exhausted as a source. The old liturgical technique of biblical patchwork is not much used by modern liturgists, but I suggest it as an enlightening exercise and offer the following sample as a beginning and a challenge.

> Come and let us return to the Lord; for he has torn, and he will heal us; he has wounded, and he will bind us up. (Hos. 6:1) Take words with you and return to the Lord (Hos. 14:3); be strong and of good courage, fear not. (Deut. 31:6) O Lord, revive your work in the midst of the years, in the midst of the years make known; in wrath remember mercy; (Hab. 3:2) that the bones which thou hast broken may rejoice. (Ps. 51:10)
> O Lord, how long shall I cry, and thou wilt not hear! even cry out to thee of violence, and thou wilt not save! (Hab. 1:2) O that my head were waters, and my eyes a fountain of tears, that I might weep day and night for the slain of the daughter of my people. (Jer. 8:23) Our bones are scattered at the grave's mouth, as when one cuts and cleaves wood on the earth. (Ps. 141:7) They cried, but

there was none to save them; to the Lord, but he answered them not. (Ps. 18:41) Ah Lord God! Wilt thou make a full end of the remnant of Israel? (Ezek. 11:13) From the end of the earth I will cry unto thee. (Ps. 61:3)

Behold, my word is like fire, says the Lord, and like a hammer that shatters rock. (Jer. 23:29) See now that I, I am he, and there is no god beside me: I kill, and I make alive; I wound, and I heal; none can deliver out of my hand. (Deut. 32:39) I form light and create darkness; I make peace and create evil; I the Lord do all these things. (Isa. 45:7)

This is my God, and I will adorn him; (Exod. 15:2) this is my sickness, and I must endure it. (Jer. 10:19) My soul thirsts for you, my flesh longs for you in a dry and thirsty land where is no water. (Ps. 63:2) Try me, O God, and seek the ground of my heart; prove me, and examine my thoughts. (Ps. 139:23) Teach us to number our days, that we may gain a heart of wisdom. Make us glad according to the days you have tormented us, for the years we have seen evil. (Ps. 90:12, 15) I am a stranger on the earth; hide not thy commandments from me. (Ps. 119:19)

For still the vision awaits its time; it hastens to the end: it will not lie. If it seem slow, wait for it: it will surely come, it will not delay. (Hab. 2;3) For the stone shall cry out of the wall, and a splinter shall answer it from the beams: (Hab. 2:11) The whole earth is full of God's glory. (Isa. 6:3)

I shall not die, but live, and declare the works of the Lord. (Ps. 118:17) He stretches out the north over the void, and hangs the earth upon nothing. (Job 26:7) Though the fig tree shall not blossom, and no fruit shall be on the vines; the labor of the olive shall fail and the fields yield no food; the flock shall be cut off from the fold and there shall be no herd in the stalls; yet will I rejoice in the Lord, I will joy in the God of my salvation. (Hab. 3:17-18.)

Again I will build thee, and thou shalt be built. (Jer. 31:3) If your outcasts be at the uttermost parts of heaven, from there will the Lord your God gather you, and from there he will fetch you. (Deut. 30:4) Behold, I will bring them from the north country, and gather them from the ends of the earth, and with them the blind and the lame, the woman with child and her that labors together; a great company shall return there. They shall come with weeping, and with supplications will I lead them; I will cause them to walk by the rivers of waters in a straight way, wherein they shall not stumble. (Jer. 31:7-8)

For this commandment that I command you today, it is not too hard for you, neither is it far off. It is not in heaven, that you should say, Who will go up for us to heaven and bring it to us, that we may hear it and do it? Neither is it beyond the sea, that you should say, Who will go over the sea for us and bring it to us, that we may hear it and do it? But the word is very nigh unto you, in your mouth and in your heart, that you may do it. (Deut. 30:11-14)

Only beware and guard yourself carefully, lest you forget the things your eyes have seen and lest they stray from your heart all the days of your life. (Deut. 4:9) And a new heart will I give you, and a new spirit will I put within you: and I will take away the stony heart out of your flesh, and I will give you a heart of flesh. (Ezek. 36:26) See, I have engraved you on the palms of my hands (Isa. 49:16); no evil shall befall you. (Ps. 91:10) And I will betroth you to me forever; I will betroth you to me in righteousness, and in judgment, and in lovingkindness, and in mercy. I will betroth you to me in faithfulness, and you shall know the Lord. (Hos. 2:21-22)

Works Cited

Grotowski, Jerzy, 1968, Towards a Poor Theatre, Holstebro, Denmark: Odin Teatrets Forlag.

Richards, Thomas, 1995, At Work with Grotowski on Physical Actions, London: Routledge.

Seligman, Adam, Robert Weller, Michael Puett, and Bennett Simon, 2008, Ritual and Its Consequences: An Essay on the Limits of Sincerity, Oxford: Oxford University Press. (Thanks to Joel Kaminsky for this reference.)

CROSSCURRENTS

RESPONSE TO CATHERINE MADSEN

Randi Rashkover

Let me begin with a "love letter to Catherine." Dear Catherine, something happened when I read your essay—something cathartic because at this point in my life I have a good 35 (OK, let's be honest), 40 years of bad synagogue experience under my belt. Sure I liked learning the prayers when I was a kid because I was good at memorization and I liked to sing, but I never enjoyed praying in synagogue. My first religious encounters were in nature. I read the transcendentalists. I became a philosopher because Emerson and Thoreau referenced Kantian idealism. I was masterful at synagogue tricks but felt nothing from them. A quick dalliance with orthodoxy during my courtship with my husband proved that I loved orthodox davening but was always seated on the wrong side of the curtain. Recent experiences with the twenty-first century "Joseph and the Amazing Technicolor Dreamcoat" school of Reform Jewish liturgical style have left me humming new tunes to the *Aleynu* after services but have done nothing for me existentially, ethically, intellectually, and even aesthetically.

So when you ask why has contemporary Jewish liturgy aimed so low? And when you insightfully announce the dubitability of the confessionalism that in liberal schuls counts for religious sentiment and devotion, I'm with you. And here is where we really must begin. Eloquently and effectively you speak of the crisis of sincerity and say, "Fundamentalist religion... is quintessentially modern and savagely sincere: it retaliates against the disruptions of modernist protest by recreating them in full force from the opposing side. The totalistic nature of sincerity, whether on the right or the left, profoundly threatens the slow, patient courtesy of liturgical world construction." Listeners might be surprised to hear you equate liberal Jewish liturgical life with "fundamentalism," but the philosophical point cannot be disregarded; sincerity of emotion is not reproducible. Liturgical practice as you and Franz Rosenzweig have taught us is predicated upon repeatable action and demands a philosophical consistency. But raw emotion is fleeting. Frequently, the charge against subjectivism in liturgy regards its failure to be rendered publically expressible. Your point regards not only the general problem of a public expression of private emotion but the deeper problem that private emotion cannot be reliably reproduced and this is in part why it cannot be publically expressed. For sincerity, you tell us, "there is never enough evidence…" Honest emotion is always just shy of credibility.

If as you argue, liturgy must be subject to evaluation, what would constitute "good liturgy?" Drawing from the classic Stanislavski guidebook for acting, you invoke the renaissance ideal of the refinement of sentiment, the education of the emotions. Liturgy you suggest presupposes the wedding of the Appollonian and the Dionysian through the inseparable nexus of form and content. And you conclude, liturgy is the setting for the production of exceptional work—exceptional because it evidences the warrant for its reproducibility over and over again and work because it must be first produced in order to be reproduced. The stakes of your mandate to "refine" our liturgical life couldn't be higher. Liturgical bouts of emotional sincerity not only undermine the very authenticity they seek to express, they also forfeit the content or what in this case is the reference to the theological "what" which you openly announce as the ultimate object of our liturgical life.

So, here is the challenge. How do we tackle it? For you, the answer lies somewhere in the transition from the subjective to the subjunctive—from the experience "as is" to the experience "as if." I see this as our first point of difference. Undoubtedly, hypothesis and imagination are crucial elements in theological work (briefly stated I believe they operate mostly to correlate between our theological desire and the apophatic limits of our theological knowledge). However, to remain consistent to your account would mean to locate evidence for reproducible action. Here, the contents of the imagination fall short since they are themselves too changeable to count as reliable data. So, where *can* we find the "what" which constitutes evidence for emotion's reproduction?

There is a deep theological reason why your call for the education of the senses within liturgical life resonates so well with my own work. Over the past five years, the core of my theological perspective has been the marriage between form and content. More specifically, I've tried to articulate the correlation between divine law—what is the structure or order established by God and the freedom of this same God to affirm the difference of human finitude and existence within this order. The God of the Hebrew Scriptures and the Jewish tradition I have argued offers the law "for us." The order of God's difference and the order of God's creation do not demand a forfeiture of our humanity but house it and justify it offering it a context within which *it* may freely live. From this perspective then, the created order operates as the expression of divine structure *and* divine redemption. The well-known biblical scholar Gerhard Von Rad argues that the biblical text offers many examples of the connection between the order of divine redemption and the freedom or care expressed in the structures of creation. Von Rad cites Isaiah 44:24: "Thus has Yahweh said, your Redeemer and the One who formed you from the womb...." It is as if for Deutero-Isaiah, the creation of the world and the redemption of Israel both exemplify the same divine dispensation."[1] We can, he suggests, find a similar nexus between God's creative acts and divine redemption throughout the psalms, citing Psalm 74 in particular, "Yet my God is from old, working salvation in the midst of the earth." A few weeks back, I was fortunate enough to give a lecture on the angel of history—on the freedom of persons within the affirmation of God's order. Such freedom registers as the proclamation of need throughout changing demands of history. Linguistically speaking, it is narrative or drama that expresses these changing desires.

Today's charge requires recourse to the notion of *law* or *structure* (rather than freedom) because it is law as structure or more directly the character of the created order which for liturgical life provides the condition for the education of the sentiments—namely their link to the evidence. In my *Freedom and Law: A Jewish-Christian Apologetics,* I speak about law as the law of the difference between the divine and the human and the order of human freedom. However, today I will focus (as noted in the reference to the psalms above) on the character of divine law within the structure of nature because objective reality in general and nature in particular afford the consistency demanded by liturgical repetition. We might state the claim this way: liturgy expresses emotion as the perception of an objective structure and in this way orders our desires. Throughout my work, I have discussed Franz Rosenzweig's conception of liturgy as the lawful housing of our historically alterable narrations. Rosenzweig's account of the annual repetition of the liturgical cycle presupposes and expresses the rest or the repose afforded the life of testimony as it is found in the order of divine freedom. If for Rosenzweig and for me, liturgical repetition acts as an eschatological limit, it only does so by referring to the realized eschatology of the order of law which it reflects.

So, having already noted the lawful character of liturgical life elsewhere, we must now understand the mechanics of how this takes place. How are sentiments educated, informed, and refined by structures so that they are reproducible and readied for liturgical expression? To ask this question is to ask about beauty. Confessionalism is ugly and theologically bankrupt but to sanctify the emotions is to beautify and restore their theological significance. Imagine what it would be like to leave synagogue having experienced something akin to an encounter with Matisse's "Red Room" or Copland's "Appalachian Spring". But again, I ask, what are the mechanics? How does a theological aesthetics operate? And rooted in a particular kind of correlation between nature's structure and our perceptions, how does such an aesthetic relate to science? What is the link between truth and beauty?

I'd like to begin by noting the uncanny resemblance between Catherine's and my interest in the education of the sentiments and the constructed conversation between a young man named Euphranor and an older man named Theocles described in an essay written by Moses Mendelssohn entitled "On Sentiments." Mendelssohn's artfully constructed sequence of letters between the two men poignantly repeats the play between the endorsement of sentiment alone and the demands of its structured and educated refinement referenced in Catherine's piece. Euphranor expresses the former position. Already at the start of his letter, we hear the passion in his tone and he says with all of the longing of a person thinking about and speaking to the object of his love, "Only yesterday I received a correspondence from you…. How often have I unfolded the letter, read, it and folded it back together."[2] Continuing on, he echoes this reverence for sentiment and speaks about the meaning of beauty. "Our happiness depends upon enjoyment and enjoyment depends upon the swift sentiment with which each beauty surprises our senses. Unhappy are those whom reason has hardened against the onset of such a surprise."[3] Beauty is the product of the sentiments and the sentiments alone! Refined or reflected upon they lose their vibrancy. "If you can, Theocles, make the feeling of beauty more lively, but guard against transforming it into barren truths… What a difference between the two claims: 'this object is beautiful' and 'this object is true'!"[4]

Undoubtedly proponents of liberal Jewish confessionalism would do well to have Euphranor as their spokesman but is he right regarding the distance between beauty and truth? I don't think so. Why are we taken aback when we listen to Copland's "Rite of Spring"? Does the beauty derive only from the emotion we feel or is it also "in the work itself" such that it may be called beautiful over time? If the beauty perdures beyond any one subjective engagement with it, is this not because the sentiment is housed within the structure of the composition? Is it not the "form" of the work that renders the sentiment possible and reproducible? And isn't therefore, the pleasure of beauty a pleasure of emotion that arises from the perception of the object? This is the position expressed by Euphranor's longed-for conversation partner, Theocles.

More than a sensuous reaction to a vague or obscure reality, aesthetic gratification Theocles tells us emerges when we perceive a multiplicity of features in an object together with an indistinct perception of the unity of these same elements. This combination of the distinct details of the structure with an indistinct perception of the unity of these elements constitutes the unique characteristic of beauty and distinguishes it from the apprehension of truth. Truth on the other hand conjoins the apprehension of the multiplicity of elements with an apprehension of the distinct unity of them as they relate to other distinct unities. Undoubtedly, intellectual apprehension is an extension of the aesthetic—though he admits that the philosopher (or scientist) who pursues it "must perhaps dispense with honor, sensual ecstasy and riches, for him they are the dust upon which he treads with his feet—preoccupied like Archimedes he says to the persecutors who stand behind him with their sword drawn: Whatever you do, don't mess up my circle!"[5] Intellectual life gratifies the mind. Beauty by contrast evokes sensuous feeling. However, both, he insists are human expressions of perfection or what I would call "structure."

Still, the beautiful differs in another way from the pursuit of science as beauty requires the failure of our perception and its clarity of apprehension. Only a multiplicity of details in an obscure unity gratifies—and it gratifies precisely because it generates longing. We can sense the beauty of the divine poetry in God's "Where were you when I laid the foundation of the earth… Who set its measurements or who stretched the line on it?" (Job 38).

So what about the theological implications of beauty? Can we make sense of Catherine's deep intuition regarding the theological loss so painfully accrued in today's turn to subjectivism? Undoubtedly, beauty registers the greatest of theological perceptions. And, I believe that it's exactly the definitional limits presented by the failure of the soul and the lawful distance between the divine and the human, which renders our perception of the divine order more theologically precious. Aesthetics is not tantamount to metaphysics and neither do they produce the dark night of the soul of apophatic theology. Structure is there—made all the more beautiful when we sense the divine more to which it points and about which we do not know but only wonder. Listen to Mendelssohn's brilliant exposition on this very point in his later "Rhapsody or Additions to the Letters on Sentiments." "I scarcely expect here the reproach that, by these considerations, I grant too much to sensuous rapture by elevating it to a perfection of the soul… We are called in this life not only to improve our powers of understanding and willing, but also to educate feeling by means of sentient knowledge and to raise the obscure impulses of the soul to a higher perfection by means of sensuous pleasure. When we neglect the latter, we act as contrary to the intentions of the creator as when we neglect the former!"[6]

Still, before closing, I must give some attention to Euphranor's response. He may be young and passionate, but he makes two good points: First: Theocles—you link the sense of beauty with the structure of perfection—but we've all been moved by that which is painful or departs from perfection or structure. Philosophically stated, if the beautiful refers to what is painful, how could it be predicated upon structure or form?

Theocles admits the credibility of Euphranor's question and introduces Mendelssohn's notion of the mixed sentiment. By "mixed sentiment," Mendelssohn means a sentiment whose object may be an imperfection or at least whose object may partially present an imperfection but which does not nullify the perfection structuring our sentiment altogether. For example, a dramatic character may undergo a terrible ordeal, but our sentiment is nonetheless drawn to the goodness and order of the character which frames our sense of sadness for his/her predicament. If anything, the beauty of the person's character emanates more powerfully from this juxtaposition to his/her unfortunate circumstances. We could apply the same principle to an example from nature and to animals or other living creatures. Still Mendelssohn argues, the perfection that structures a mixed sentiment need not derive from the object at all but may derive from the form of representation imposed upon it. Structure in other words may emerge from nature, but it may also emerge from art—from the lines and letters and words that we craft and use to inform our sentiments. In this case not, it's not the pain that constitutes the pleasure, but the beauty of the representation of it by the artist. Undoubtedly, beauty presupposes artifice—it encases experience and imposes a crafted distance from it without which the sense would not be beautiful but horrible or terrifying or sorrowful. Tragedy promotes sympathy, not empathy. Certainly, Jewish liturgical literature offers many examples of this sort of representation and understood within this context we must absolutely guard participants from the desire to "relate" to the representation. To appropriate, it is to psychologize it and render it unusable for liturgical performance. Undoubtedly, this raises a challenging issue since we know that it is the very mandate of Jewish memory that the contemporary community sees itself as linked to the community of the past. Still, it is my contention that if we appreciate the existential, theological, and hermeneutical requirements of this kind of collective memory, then we must question whether the enactment and development of it is the proper activity of liturgical life. I'd like to suggest that it falls within the purview of collective text study instead.

And yet, with this question, we come to my final point of discussion: Euphanor's second and more powerful challenge to Theocles. What happens when we confront a sentiment that cannot be refined—a sentiment so devastating, so painful that it cannot be rendered beautiful without being undermined? Doesn't the reference to the perfection of nature or representation challenge our right to sentiments that cannot be represented without significant cost? Implicit in the challenge are two separate questions: the first is whether or not persons really experience these sorts of sentiments and even if they do, do these sorts of sentiments endure or do they vanish (a suggestion Mendelssohn makes in response to Euphanor). The second question is: if persons do experience evil or the radical imperfection of the world, what place would the expression of such sentiment have in liturgy? Because it would take a long time to answer question one, let's assume the answer is "yes" and consider question two. In an introduction to a volume I edited called *Liturgy Time and the Politics of Redemption,* I spoke of the particular character of petitionary prayer exemplified most dramatically by Hannah—a woman whose prayer was deemed exemplary by the rabbis. From there, I further referenced Rabbi Joseph Soloveitchik's appreciation for the value of petitionary prayer. Unfortunately, I also noted Soloveitchik's contrary insistence upon the idea that only *halakha* defines the bounds of our needs and determines which are rightful and "normal" and which are not. Didn't, I asked, Soloveitchik's emphasis upon the mediation of need through law overly determine the freedom of our range of emotion and desire? If so does not the education of the sentiments within liturgical life operate similarly? If it does how then do we reconcile prayer as the service of the heart *and* the education of the sentiments—an education we so desperately need for the sake of nothing less than our devotion to God?

Notes

1. Von Rad, Gerhard, *From Genesis to Chronicles: Explorations in Old Testament Theology* (Minneapolis: Augsburg Fortress Press, 2005), p. 180.
2. Mendelssohn, Moses, "On Sentiments" in *Philosophical Writings*, ed. Daniel O. Dahlstrom (Cambridge: Cambridge University Press, 1997), p. 9.
3. Mendelssohn, "On Sentiments," p. 9.
4. Ibid. 13.
5. Ibid. 16.
6. Mendelssohn, Moses, "Rhapsody or additions to the Letters on Sentiments" in *Philosophical Writings*, p. 140.

CROSSCURRENTS

RESPONSE TO CATHERINE MADSEN— GOD AS CRITERION OF JEWISH LITURGY

Steven Kepnes

Catherine Madsen has brought up important issues regarding a renaissance of Jewish liturgy in liberal Jewish communities of the twenty-first century. Certainly, we are seeing great creativity in Jewish liturgy. There are many sparks flying and many new songs being sung. Yet Madsen seems to worry whether or not the sparks are strange fires and the new songs mere jingles of the moment rather than soulful melodies that arise from the struggle to contact God and that, once heard, cannot be forgotten. Madsen asks whether these liturgical innovations can have staying power since they seem to be invented anew with each liturgical occasion and the central criteria for the liturgy is the sincerity of the liturgist and the intensity of the liturgical experience. She juxtaposes these criteria with more traditional Jewish ones: "knowing before whom you stand" and doing the liturgical act to fulfill a mitzvah or divine command whether one fully understands it or not.

By reminding us of the form and goals of Orthodox liturgy, Madsen is not calling for a return to Orthodoxy. I think that she truly shares the goals of contemporary liturgical renaissance in liberal Judaism that will make more space for women and others that the old rite excludes. She also knows that when liturgy is done only as rote with no passion, as we often see in Orthodoxy, it can be deadly boring and spiritually vacuous.

What Madsen does seem to want in the contemporary renaissance in Jewish liturgy is more serious Jewish and liturgical thinking beforehand, more respect for the scope and ultimate religious goal of liturgical acts, and more continuity to the traditions of the past.

In my terms, what I see Madsen doing is to bring theological concerns to liturgy. Therefore, what is central for me in Madsen's critique of the frivolousness of much contemporary liberal Jewish liturgy are the words. *Da lifnei mi atah omed*, "know before whom you stand." Knowing that you stand before the One God of Israel, before the Holy One and God of the Universe, clarifies what is central to all Jewish liturgy, be it the ritual breaking of bread by the individual or the complex choreography surrounding the taking out and reading the Torah in the synagogue. In liturgy, the liturgist stands before God. In liturgy, the liturgist praises, thanks, blesses, and asks forgiveness and mercy from God. Everything is done in Jewish liturgy for the sake of God and before God and God is the ultimate criteria and judge of the quality, sincerity, and intensions of liturgy. God, not mom and pop, not grandma and zeidi, not one's friends, and not even the Rabbi, are the judges and bestowers of mercy that one seeks in Jewish liturgy.

The contemporary Jewish liturgist, Cantor Tamar Havilio of Hebrew Union College Jerusalem, has summed up the central problem with much contemporary progressive Jewish liturgy nicely. She traces the problem back to the time when the Rabbi and Cantor placed themselves up front of the synagogue and turned around to face the congregation instead remaining in the middle of the congregation and praying with them toward the ark that represents God. When the Rabbi and Cantor pray toward the congregation, the symbolism is clear. Rabbi and Cantor are praying to the congregation and not God. Rabbi and Cantor are there to serve the congregation and not to lead the congregation to serve God. Rabbi and Cantor are there to entertain the congregation. And the synagogue service becomes a kind of a concert or lecture rather than a collective ritual of service of the heart to God.

Since the Rabbi and Cantor represent God to the community, we could easily draw out a further implication. God, himself, must serve the congregation; the congregation does not serve God. Like the Rabbi, God is always chasing and searching for Jews; Jews need not search for Him. The synagogue service then becomes a kind of consumerist fare to be tried out and judged by how it meets certain vague spiritual and esthetic sensibilities of congregants. Jews, then, through their own wishes, desires, and money, judge the prayer service and the Rabbi and the Cantor, and they similarly judge God.

"God," they say, "God, show yourself to me." "God, prove to me that you are real. Tell me why I should believe in you." In other words, "God, my problem relating to you, praying to you, speaking to you, is your problem, you fix it, I cannot." Like the contemporary parent in the consumer society, God can only bestow gifts; he can only give "unconditional positive regard." He cannot judge and he cannot make demands.

This, of course, changes the most basic equation of the relation of God to Israel in the Torah. For in the Torah, it is God who has neither single nor simple demands but complex demands, 613 demands, demands that are liturgical, moral, civil, and environmental. In the Torah, Israel must give animal sacrifices daily to keep the holiness and order that God put in the world when he created it. Without the sacrificial offerings, Israel would have no access to God and the world would collapsing into chaos. In the rabbinic tradition, the synagogue comes to substitute for the sacrificial altar, but still the sense of preserving holiness and order in the world remains as collective liturgical prayer takes the place of animal sacrifices. So here we have the basic purpose of Jewish liturgy, to preserve the order and holiness in God's created world and to provide an access of Jews to God. Innovators in Jewish liturgy would be aided if they kept these goals in mind for they are serious, collective, theological, even cosmic goals, that go well beyond the simple needs of Jewish individuals for spiritual entertainment or esthetic pleasure.

Madsen mentions that liturgy is a kind of sacred theater. Sacred theater differs from secular theater in that the audience participates in the theater. I think that thinking about Jewish liturgy as sacred theater is helpful since it clarifies that what the liturgy is about is not the stories and experiences of the participants but about the enactment of roles and the articulation of lines that have already been determined beforehand. Moses Mendelssohn liked to see Jewish ceremonies or liturgies as a matter of following a script. The script is given by God and the tradition and the goal of the community is to play the script in the best way that it can.

We can think of the Passover Seder as providing a script for Jewish families to play. In this play, the goal is to relive the Exodus story. The goal of the story is to first transform participants back into slaves by having them eat the "bread of affliction," the *matzah*, as their ancestors did. In the next stage of the liturgy, the Seder aims to bring the participants "out of bondage," first to experience physical freedom and then to know a new type of spiritual freedom through bondage to God. Bondage to God is understood as accepting God's commands and mitsvot and these can be understand and a series of additional scripts for actions that Israel must carry out.

If the overall structure and theological goals of the Passover Seder are kept in mind, the Seder allows for a great amount of creativity and innovation. Every family can develop their own particular Seder provided that they follow the basic structure and fulfill the overall goals. Since the Passover Seder is one of the most widely celebrated Jewish liturgies, and since most Jews are aware that they are allowed to innovate with this liturgy, I would offer it as a model for how creative liturgy for the liberal community could occur.

But for the innovative Seder to be a model for how a Jewish religious renaissance could occur, I would recall once again Catherine Madsen's suggestion. *Da lifnei mi atah omed.* Know before whom you stand. This indeed is the demand that Catherine Madsen puts to the contemporary Jewish community as it attempts to accomplish a Jewish renaissance. Without this knowledge, the knowledge of God, no renaissance worthy of the more than three thousand-year-old tradition of Judaism will be possible. With this knowledge, which as Madsen suggests, is a deep and intimate form of knowing that is far more than rational acknowledgement, a criterion for all Jewish liturgical creativity becomes clear. Does this liturgical innovation lead to more honor, respect, more thanks, more blessing, and a deeper and more intimate relationship to the One God, the Holy One, Creator of the universe, Revealer of the Torah and Redeemer of Israel and the world. If so, it is to be approved, if not, rejected.

CROSSCURRENTS

RESPONSE TO CATHERINE MADSEN, "A HEART OF FLESH: BEYOND 'CREATIVE LITURGY'"

Leah Hochman

In her critique of contemporary efforts to have a "liturgical experience" rather than to perform "a liturgical act," Catherine Madsen argues that "liturgy shares with theater the need for aesthetic and psychological coherence." One need not—and should not—mistake the intensity of feeling for authentic liturgical action; rather, a liturgy that can be sustained and can sustain one and/or others beyond a singular moment requires a relevance that can represent feeling and intentionality while maintaining an integrity of response and meaning. That integrity must include not only good writing but good sentiment and a refinement of spiritual intelligence. The silliness or fluff that can so often characterize "creative liturgy" is an inept substitute for the deeper, more emotional resonant liturgy of the more traditional sort. As she reminds us, "the leopards in Kafka's parable break into the temple so dependably that they finally become part of the ritual, but there are kavvanot that will never be more than irritants no matter how often we hear them."

Her critique resonates on several levels even as I find myself wondering whether I agree with it. Perhaps my own response has to do with my current position at the Hebrew Union College-Jewish Institute of Religion, where so many of my students engage in the sort of creative endeavor that Madsen finds tedious and unfulfilling. But the seminary students are—as I often like to remind them and myself—in a sort of "teaching hospital" where their attempts at writing, employing, testing new (and old) liturgy are sanctioned in the very kind of workshop experience with which Madsen opens her comments. Dropping stitches during *tefilah* at HUC is sanctioned if only because it is far better to do so in an environment of continual learning and constructive feedback than in the operating room of a solo congregation where one is the only operator. Not that I do not squirm uncomfortably when the experimentation veers too far off course for me or runs dangerously close to summer camp *beit knesset* antics. And yet the rabbinic students and their congregations know there is more to creative liturgy than simply the happenstance, "kindergarten" dilettantish sincerity that Madsen describes. While I cannot argue against the knowledge that some new prayers reverberate with a kind of cloying and artless parvenu-ishness, it would be unfair to forget that the current, ongoing shift in liberal liturgical circles has opened prayerful avenues in complex, interesting, and multi-sensory ways.

Her opening gambit about repetition posits for me the question of whether her criticism of liturgical experimentation is an issue about simple repetition or a deeper query regarding what kind of repetition actually resonates with us. The maligned Mary Oliver poem aside, I find myself wondering, what are the differences between Oliver's poetry and Kafka's leopards? And who is "us"? What moves an academic participant in a Jewish liturgical moment may not be the same as what moves other actors and participants in Jewish prayer (that old joke about two Jews and three shuls comes immediately to mind), but it references the range of what could possibly force people to think beyond their own experience and reference points. How much must we know before we know whether liturgy moves us appropriately? Do we judge the sparseness of the biblical language the same way we value the flowering poetry of the Psalms that makes up the *psukei d'zimra*? Madsen is correct in suggesting that the majority of liberal congregants do not have the linguistic facility in Hebrew to open and access the glorious beauty of many of the prayers that make up the traditional liturgy. Why do we respond to it the way/s in which we do? It may be that if people did understand those most personal prayers made public sentiment—or when they do—the theological messages imbedded within the traditional liturgy would not speak to the ways in which individual Jews understand or appreciate the divine. Not all traditional liturgies make good liturgy; just because it is old does not mean it speaks to my "private loyalty" or my "public allegiances." And that is the dilemma with which I struggle. The leopards crash into the Temple without the encouragement of the priests but become ritualized because of the way they affect the process of prayer. But in the attempt to mimic theological investment without evoking a real, Jewish engagement with the divine bad poetry or weak rhetoric skirt making a mockery of the endeavor. How does one affect prayer meaningfully?

That may be the issue. Madsen reminds us that "renaissance work" requires "an exuberant and disciplined pursuit of high competence" and not inexact, inaccurate efforts that fumble in their attempt to give birth to a new set of prayers that pay homage to tradition while going beyond that tradition. One need not have an advanced degree in liturgy to know how the pieces of the morning service flow together or that the *aleinu* seeks a reification of Jewish superiority through divine justification; if one wants to add to (or subtract from) either, one must do so knowingly, respectfully, not willy-nilly but with a vested interest in renewing the deep seated religiosity of the prayer. For those who are participants but not authors of such attempts, the effects are successful in the sensory experiences new prayer can evoke. As a means of activating the soul liturgy seeks to include—through description or through implementation—the senses. What has been so remarkable to me as I see rabbinical students master the traditional liturgy of old, the new liturgies of liberal and Reform Judaisms, and their own attempts at making prayers that bear repetition (and can be borne repeating) is the impact of music. Even more specifically, in Jewish prayer, a sung Psalm beats a read poem. The auditory component to prayer can make or break the experience of praying in a community. Madsen dwells on the repetitive actions related to prayer without calling attention to the clout of the tune in which such liturgy is felt, expressed, and shared. Of course, not every refrain hits its mark. There is a very fine line distinguishing a song fest from a worship service. And many times that line is crossed (innocently, because of the joy of the song or more intentionally, as a way of distraction). But in employing the field of the repetitive auditory experience, the reification of ritual meaning can find the target of personal meaning: even for the dreaded elitist, a tune can open the heart in ways language can only follow.

The ritual, liturgical, repetitive power of the *shir* (poem and song) has come into sharper focus for me recently. I hesitate to use her as an example since her legacy bears the burden of being overexposed (and thus subject to a different kind of criticism), yet the power of Debbie Friedman's innovations in liturgical text cannot—should not—be overlooked. Perhaps more than any other single individual, Friedman's songs have changed liberal Jewish liturgy and in so doing have changed the way that Jews of all denominations hear and see the landscape of Jewish texts. As an example, look to her song "Lekhi Lakh" in which the command to Abraham to go (lekh lekha) echoes the command of the lover in Song of Songs (lekhi lakh) and engages the singer of the song not just to marry the two biblical texts together but to re-imagine divine commands as female and male, as coming and going, as human calls and as divine charters. It is a deeply theological song with complex music that invites the individual to reach higher notes when one may want to turn away or down and that engages the biblical text directly while making that text have contemporary meaning. And, because it is sung a summer camps and youth group events—and yes, at Reform temples—the song might be dismissed without real consideration. One might say the same about Friedman's reborn versions of *mi khamokha*, *misheberakh*, and Zechariah 4:6.

That, I think, is the challenge that Madsen sets out for me. The critique of creative liturgy can no more be knee jerk or trite than our acceptance of what seems to be authentic. She charges us to be as careful in our evaluation of the psychological and aesthetic experience—both intellectual and sensory—of new liturgical efforts as we are appreciative of the good liturgy of tradition. Part of the artistry of the renaissance in Jewish prayer comes not only from *avodah sheb'lev* (the "service of the heart") but also from *hokhmei lev* (the "wisdom of the heart"). I do believe, as Madsen offhandedly remarks, that the function of liberal Judaism is other than "relaxing the standards of observance"; in allowing the texts and the craft of biblical, rabbinic, medieval, and modern liturgical efforts to be handled by non-experts, liberal Judaism lets those who long for a way to match (Jewish) words to (Jewish) deeds to get their hands dirty doing so. That willingness to *try*, to work through the various feelings to find that "something there" that Grotowski saw in Richards' action, is the gift that liberal Judaism gives to each of us. As the rabbis say, we may not finish the work but neither can we desist from it.

CROSSCURRENTS

RESPONSE TO CATHERINE MADSEN'S PAPER, "A HEART OF FLESH: BEYOND 'CREATIVE LITURGY'"

Caroline Rody

The unexpected ending of Catherine Madsen's paper stuns us with an extended experience of the strong poetry of the Bible. Given that "A Heart of Flesh" performs its critique of liberal liturgy by analogy with good and bad art, mostly in the form of theater, and because I come to this panel from the perspective of literary study, I want to speak about the extent to which she is and is not talking about a preference for good over bad writing.

What makes good writing? It is notoriously hard to say. It was Emily Dickinson who famously remarked, "If I feel physically as if the top of my head were taken off, I know that is poetry." More practical and somewhat more objective criteria can be assembled; one scholar who recently attempted to catalog the characteristics of the best poems made a good list: "creative daring, figurative reach, verbal dexterity, formal skill, historical responsiveness, social significance, psychological complexity, emotional richness, and the inventive engagement with" other written and unwritten verbal texts (Ramazani 2003, xxix). But the very length of this list suggests that the problem of defining literary quality could be revisited endlessly.

For even to ask the question what makes writing good is to raise thorny issues. Any evaluative criteria will inevitably carry biases; they will differ in different moments, in different schools of thought, among different readerly populations. A circular reasoning may govern our evaluations, in which our unexamined values serve to identify greatness in a poem or a prose text, and that discovered greatness then confirms our preconceived notions. And so in an examination like Madsen's of "creative liturgy," one could argue that a preexisting bias toward biblical poetry, toward texts coded as sacred, and toward traditional liturgical structures, patterns, and language would make it unlikely that any New Age liturgical text could sound just right.

But to respond to Madsen's paper only on this level is to miss its point that what makes poetry good in liturgy is not the same as what makes it good under a tree or in the classroom. The ritual experience, she suggests, involves a kind of work—as in *avodah*, service—that is not meant to reap instantaneous rewards, but "yields its relevance gradually through participation." It is a doing, she says, a "slow, patient courtesy of world construction," and the language of ritual needs to work, too, to help us do that work of construction, of discovery, the discovery of a "private loyalty" which "we want to be held to."

Madsen's is then an instrumental or extrinsic critique of liturgical writing rather than an intrinsic one; the question is not so much, "is the writing good in itself?", but "what does it make happen?" Is it good for the purpose it is supposed to serve? Of course, literary readers do sometimes work with instrumental criteria as well; Dickinson, too, wants the writing to do something to her, to take the top of her head off. And when modern readers say we want literature to offer "figurative reach," or "emotional richness," suggestiveness or multivalence, we are also talking about something we want the language to do for us. We want it to send us off working to grasp its fullest resonances; or we want it to enable us to think in a variety of ways about it, at once.

How does the poetic language that Madsen prefers for use in the synagogue do its particular kind of thing, make its particular change in us? Most obviously, the too-easy poem (represented in her paper by poor Mary Oliver) renders its meaning well once and lacks luster afterward; therefore, it stops making us do the work, while the biblical lines she quotes are richer, more demanding, more re-readable in the sense that they continually probe us to enter them anew. But it is important that they do this not through figurative difficulty, as in some of the most challenging or obscure modernist poems, but rather, as demonstrated in the striking figurative clarity of Madsen's biblical patchwork, through what she beautifully calls "wounding language."

This phrase, while it oddly recalls again the top of Dickinson's head, names that element in biblical poetry of dramatic human struggle, of longing and awe before God; that vigorously physical, elemental imagery of body and nature by which the Bible articulates separation from and promised connection to God—images of tearing and wounding and rebinding, of breaking bones that rejoice again, of fire and rock, stone, splinter, and beams, fig and olive, flock and water, killing and making alive, light and darkness, peace and evil, weeping, thirst and torment, teaching and proving, betrothal, rebuilding, gathering, flesh and spirit, and knowledge. To read these words is to be thrust into a physical universe stirred and animated by God, a world that ripples around a divine power, responds to it, aches and cries for it. Reciting such lines together, we synagogue attendees are invited to place ourselves, own intimate inner lives within this dramatically energized landscape. Entering into this linguistic world, one feels, somebody has already described my world and my life better than I could. Somebody seems to know me. In this landscape, I might come to know that somebody.

Perhaps you noticed that at the end of the list of visceral terms I read is the term "knowledge." Madsen's biblical patchwork begins "Come let us return to the Lord," and ends, "and you shall know the Lord." In her vision, it is the return, over and over, into a poetic world animated by God, that can gradually help the ritual participant construct a path to a very private, difficult, earned knowing.

Work Cited

Ramazani, Jahan, 2003, Preface, in Jahan Ramazani, Richard Ellmann, and Robert O'Clair, eds., *The Norton Anthology of Modern and Contemporary Poetry* (3rd ed., Vol. 1), New York: Norton, Print.

CROSSCURRENTS

CATHERINE MADSEN RESPONDS

I am most grateful for these five attentive—and very differently attentive—responses to my essay.

Vanessa Ochs's anthropological approach is appropriately open-ended and nonjudgmental, and raises entertainingly a number of criteria for evaluating liturgy. Conspicuously absent from these criteria—because they are not the province of anthropology, and because, not being on the seder plate of most contemporary liturgists, they cannot even be studied as other people's criteria—are aesthetic competence and moral weight. Naturally these are contentious factors, but some combination of them is necessary for a ritual to gain currency and staying power across generations. Possibly the central question of liturgy is "What kind of people are we trying to make?" The anthropologist can just wait and see what happens, but the liturgical innovator must either have some instinct or learn to take some thought for consequences.

Steven Kepnes takes a harder theological line than mine; I do not insist that it is God "before whom you stand." I do insist that liturgy be congruent with our experience of obligation. In the most important moral sense, it may well be mom and pop, grandma and zeidi, one's friends and the rabbi, among others, before whom we stand—not in their capacity as familiar faces and known quantities, but in their capacity as the stranger, the Other. The vulnerability of the face, as Levinas says, commands us; if we are never sure whether we stand before God, we stand always before the poor and destitute, and before the nakedness and fragility of every face we encounter. A case could be made that the service leader should indeed face and serve the congregation. Yet I agree with Kepnes and Cantor Feffer that in practice this puts a false emphasis on the leader, who cannot genuinely serve every face in the group at once and is therefore put in the position of a performer, a "personality." To scale back the personality, to return it to the plain offer *hineni*, "here am I," it is helpful for the leader to address the face we cannot see.

Leah Hochman has been generous with my ingratitude; the intuitions of an insistent layperson must seem to a professor in a rabbinical seminary to originate in left field. I agree with Hochman about the power of a good tune, and as a service leader I seek tunes and pursue them; in fact it was music that brought me over the line of conversion after several years of philosophical ambivalence. Still, a tune can misdirect one's experience of a prayer. If the best-known Aleinu tune were based on something more reflective than "Itsy-Bitsy Spider," it would convey something more complex than a "reification of Jewish superiority through divine justification." Is it a convert's naïveté that reads the Aleinu in a minor key, as a resolute acceptance of a difficult and tragic fate and a difficult God? The Itsy-Bitsy tune is finally a little endearing for its sheer inadequacy to the occasion, but that does not quite excuse it. The heart-opening properties of the late Debbie Friedman's songs are best appreciated by hearts that open easily, while hearts seeking to be broken and contrite will find in her music no hard edges to break on. The interesting juxtaposition of *Lech lecha* and *Lechi lach* becomes unfortunately vacuous when set to a tune that recalls the slighter pop efforts of 1958. We await a pop-inflected liturgical music with the moral urgency—indivisible from the aesthetic urgency of instruments, lyrics and voices—of the Four Tops' "Reach Out, I'll Be There" (whose meaning, not incidentally, is *hineni*).

Randi Rashkover's complex and wide-ranging discussion offers many points of entry. I am agnostic on the relationship of truth and beauty, at least as Mendelssohn presents it: his Euphranor, like Jane Austen's Marianne Dashwood or Kierkegaard's aesthete in *Either/Or*, is an aesthetic consumer, not a producer, and has only the dimmest sense of the role of judgment in artistic creation. What the authors of *Ritual and Its Consequences* mean by "as if" is not at all this kind of free-floating imagination flitting from flower to flower: they mean the imaginative structure presented by a particular liturgy. In Jewish ritual practice, we behave "as if" we were commanded, and so rehearse the self-discipline, care, and justice we are commanded to create as concrete realities in the world. Rashkover's final questions about painful and devastating sentiments are answered, it seems to me, by the structure of the Psalms, among other biblical texts: *hadrat kodesh*, the beauty of holiness, not only encompasses but depends upon the confrontation with evil and radical imperfection. The redemptive force of biblical language, as I tried to show in my selection of texts, draws its strength precisely from the energy of the evils it opposes. The weakness of much contemporary liturgy stems from the absence of this dialectic.

Caroline Rody, in prose of some elegance, has grasped my essential point: that liturgical language is itself *avodah*, obligation. Its expertise has a purpose. It is—I borrow the term from Charles Williams's novel *Shadows of Ecstasy*, where it is meant partly, but only partly, satirically—"applied literature": concentrated and compelling writing that intends not simply to keep us turning the pages, or even to make us think subtly and feel strongly, but literally to compel us. Liturgy is physically, emotionally, and intellectually calibrated to move us to certain modes of attention and of action—reliably, through reflexes founded in the deepest places of our subjectivity. "The I," says Levinas in *Totality and Infinity*, "is a privilege and an election....The morality called inward and subjective exercises a function which universal and objective law cannot exercise, but which it calls for." The imaginative training involved in liturgical practice is a sort of *techne* for the moral imagination generally. As if knowing the right thing to do will make you want to do the right thing.

CROSSCURRENTS

LAW AS LYRIC, LYRIC AS STAR TREK: A READING OF KOL NIDRE

Eric Murphy Selinger

Some years ago, I decided to stop coming to Yom Kippur services—at least, to the services for adults. This wasn't just a matter of scheduling or comfort, although I'll admit that the 90-minute children's service I took up instead has a good deal to offer on both counts, including a live performance of the Book of Jonah, complete with a four-foot cardboard fish and a pint-sized female God in a cotton-ball beard. I decided to stop coming because, frankly, I didn't see the point. When the second intifada broke out, right in the middle of the Days of Awe, the responses I heard to it before Yom Kippur were just the same as those I heard after the holiday. Those who blamed the Palestinians before, blamed them afterward. Those who blamed Israel, blamed Israel. Those who didn't know what to do, or say, or think, remained confused. For my friends, for "my people" as I saw them on the news, and, most of all, for myself, 25 hours of fasting and prayer hadn't done a thing. At which point, bring on the cotton balls.

My years among the kinderlach haven't taught me much about politics. They have, however, let me step back from the text of the Yom Kippur services a while—let me see it freshly, and not through that scrim of disappointment. In this essay I want to look at one part of that service rather closely, the way I might look at a poem, with an eye to what it says and does and can teach us about how to make the holiday do its work. I want to look at "Kol Nidre."

The first thing to notice about Kol Nidre is, I think, how very strange it is—and strange in a variety of ways. Let's start with the invocation, those first few lines we rise at, setting the stage:

> By authority of the court on high
> and by the authority of this court below,
> with divine consent and with the consent of this congregation
> we hereby declare that it is permitted to pray
> with those who have transgressed.

Notice how, right from the start, we're in the world of make-believe, of performance, just as much as we would be at any children's service. We rise and speak, and two courts appear: one visible, played by us, and one invisible, echoing our actions. These two courts, of heaven and earth, are in concord—neither sits (or stands) in judgment on the other.

This is, then, not simply an invocation, but an incantation: a set of words that make things happen. "With the consent of XYZ" is, in fact, a common formula in Jewish folk religion, a start to exorcisms and other forms of counter-magic. Joshua Trachtenberg, in *Jewish Magic and Superstition*, quotes several spells like this:

> By the authority of the Heavenly Court and by the authority of the Earthly Court, with the consent of the Holy One, blessed by He, and with the consent of Elijah...we release and annul and cancel all the oaths that have been sworn...by every angel and demon and all the angels of destruction and demonic winds against Israel, . . .

> With the consent of the heavenly and earthly courts, of our sacred Torah, of the great and small Sanhedrins, and of this holy congregation, we release N son of N from all the curses, maledictions, oaths, vows...uttered in his home or directed against him, be they his own curses or the curses of others against his person, etc.

So: we start with magic. Not the binding of demons or dissolution of curses, or even the undoing of an oath; that will come later. Rather, we make a gesture of permission. "It is permitted to pray/with those who have transgressed." What magic does this declaration perform?

The first thing it does, at least to my suspicious mind, is raise a few doubts about the rest of you. What do I know, after all, about what you've been up to for the last twelve months? Next, it calls to mind my own self-doubts. If you knew what I'd been up to all last year—if you knew what I'd been up to last week—would you really want to pray with me? But of course, the prayer doesn't say "want to"; it says "permitted to"—and this, in turn, suggests a truly scary counterfactual scenario. What would it be like *not* to be permitted to pray with transgressors, even if we wanted to? It's not hard to imagine those in our community we'd most like to shun, to expel, to shrug off and declare outside the fold. Those settlers. Those leftists. Those messianists, whatever the Moshiach they profess. Those whose vision of Judaism most grates against my own. It doesn't take me long to muster a minyan I wouldn't pray with, *couldn't* pray with, in good conscience—and I've often thought there should be more of this sort of private excommunication, in every faith community, by us liberals, just to show those people how we feel. At the thought, though, that I would not be *permitted* to pray with them, or anyone, by a court here or elsewhere, my heart rebels—just as strongly as it would at anyone saying he or she was forbidden to pray with me. As Sarah Ironson says in Tony Kushner's "Angels in America," a Jew "*darf ringen mit zain Libm Nomen*" [should struggle with the Almighty], since "*Azoi toot a Yid*" [it's what a Jew does, or—as Kushner's Rabbi Isidor Chemelwitz spins the translation—"It's the Jewish way"].

Not even God, says this invocation, can stop me from praying with you.

If this act of rebellion returns us to what the poet Robert Duncan calls "a place of first permission"—a gathering in which all the "transgressors" are consciously, defiantly included—the text of the Kol Nidre proper specifies the sort of transgression that the service has in mind. Consider the opening lines:

> All vows, prohibitive vows, oaths, vows of dedication, konam-vows, konas-vows, and equivalent terms that we have vowed, sworn, declared, and imposed upon ourselves...

But let's stop there. What sort of language, and what language game, is this?

At first glance, it seems a quintessential scrap of legalese, the sort of language one's eyes glaze over at in insurance policies. "All vows, prohibitive vows, oaths, vows of declaration, konam-vows, konas-vows and equivalent terms," erga omnes, res judicata, the party of the first part hereunto. What a delicious contradiction lies in our pouring out our hearts in such phrases—it's like going to the opera to hear Kiri Te Kanawa sing her contract, not "O Mio Babbino Caro." This may be the strangeness of the whole halakhic system, law and passion juxtaposed, which Kol Nidre allows progressive Jews to hear and feel a few minutes every year.

Of course, when you're just listening to the Aramaic, you don't hear the legalese. What you hear, instead, is a list. For me, as a reader of poetry, such a list calls to mind not only other lists and litanies in the service—"Yitgadal v'yitkadash" and so on in the Kaddish, for example—but also the magical way that catalogs work in poets like Whitman. The impulse to catalog, says Richard Wilbur, often embodies "a longing to possess the whole world, and to praise it"; and if we don't hear praise this time (as we do in the Kaddish), we certainly find that world-encompassing, world-conjuring desire. We live, this list suggests, in a *promissory world*; our heads and lives are full of oaths and vows and promises, not primarily to one another (none of these five is a vow to another person), but to ourselves. We swear to God we'll do this, and not do that, call Mom once a week and never speak to that in-law again—those are mine, and I'll bet you have your own. Such vows make up, these lines suggest, a fair chunk of our constant, self-admonishing, self-correcting interior monologue, and at this moment of intersection between heaven and earth, we are asked to imagine what that monologue would sound like if someone had actually been listening.

Imagine if we were actually to be held responsible for all of those vows—and, worse, held responsible for those of the rest of the community! Forget praying with me; who'd want to be seen with me? (I never write, I never call…) Just as we do with the list of abstract sins in the "Al Chet Shechatanu," we are asked to call up vivid instances in our own minds, phrase by phrase, fleshing out each abstraction we utter with a mortifying, emotionally vivid example. Only thus, like a lyric poem, can we bring the prayer to life.

I've been speaking so far of vows from last year, and indeed, that's what the oldest texts of Kol Nidre refer to. The classical Western Sephardi formulation, from Spain and Portugal, preserves this formulation: "All nidrei, esarei, shivuei, charamei, niduyei, hunamei, kunachei, and kunasei which we have vowed, sworn, declared, pronounced, and imposed upon ourselves from the previous Yom Kippur until this Yom Kippur which has come upon us in peace," the rabbi begins, and the congregation responds: "regarding them all, let them be erased and forgiven."

Now, despite my usual preference for the Sephardi take on things—romanzas and not klezmer, rice and beans for Pesach, stuffed grape leaves and not gefilte fish as Jewish food—I must say that, when it comes to Kol Nidre, the Ashkenazi version seems to me vastly superior. Again, it's for the strangeness. Listen to the language carefully:

> All vows, etc. etc., that we have vowed, sworn, declared, and imposed upon ourselves from this day of atonement until the next day of atonement, may it come upon us for good...

Let's stop there, before the strangeness can slip by.

In these Ashkenazi phrases, we encounter a very slippery bit of rhetoric. We speak in the past tense (we *have vowed*) about the future (from this Yom Kippur until the next). We look back on something, with regret, that we haven't even done yet! For a moment, if we pay attention, we're all like Captain Picard from *Star Trek: The Next Generation*, trapped in a Class-D temporal distortion; or, to be more serious, it's as though we have, as we utter the prayer, a timeless, simultaneous perspective on ourselves in the past and the coming year.

Remember what the text just said. It's not just that we'll be tempted to make these vows. It's not that we will make them. We've already vowed, sworn, declared, pronounced, and the rest, and have already failed. There's a tension here, both grammatical and psychological: a tension that is barely resolved as we shift into the present tense request of the next sentence (let them all be released, forgiven, erased, null and void) and then into our chutzpadik declaration that the request has in fact already been answered: "they are not valid nor are they in force."

In Star Trek terms, we have, with this last declaration, effectively closed the temporal anomaly. We wipe out our anticipated regret by changing the past through a daring raid on the future. (I think I even saw that episode.) But in the world of Yom Kippur, the text suggests, our mission isn't done. There are still a few phrases to go.

As a reader of poetry, I have always loved the final phrases of Kol Nidre. This braid of paradoxes—our vows are not vows, our oaths are not oaths—is another intersection of magical and legal thinking, of liturgy and poetry. What could it really mean, after all, to make such a declaration? If we take the phrases seriously, not as halakhah, but as an emotional truth, they sound to me something like this:

We know what vows are, really, or ought to be. We know how they bind; we know how they compel; we know the magic of words. We also know that whatever our vows and oaths are, they're not *that*. At this moment, when we see ourselves through the eyes of that heavenly court, we're really not very impressive. This is why I don't like the comforting historical legend that Kol Nidre dates from the days after the expulsion from Spain, an apologetic account of the prayer which pegs its pathos to the secret Jews who were forced to vow things they'd of course regret.

But Kol Nidre isn't about ourselves as victims. That's too easy. It's about ourselves as endlessly inventive self-deceivers, living on the credit of our oaths and vows. Faced with judgment, Kol Nidre suggests, we *will* swear that this year we'll do better. We've all been kids; we all think we can promise our way to forgiveness. As adults, though, we also know that we are going to forget those vows or regret them, likely as not. In fact, the text doesn't say "likely as not"; it says, we *will* regret them, we *do* regret them; our vows are no vows at all. In the eyes of Kol Nidre, we are all, for a moment, Calvinists, believers both in predestination and in, as the Puritans called it, our "total depravity," an utter incompetence to improve. Like spiders held over a fire, as Jonathan Edwards once wrote, we are dangled over the abyss of our own *nebbishkeit*. And if that won't get us to ask for help—from God or each other, transgressors or not—what will?

It's not often we Jews get to speak and feel so poorly about ourselves, either collectively or one by one. "Lord, I am not worthy to receive you" is not part of our liturgy; on Shabbat we welcome the Queen to our table without so much as a blush. But if we are indeed asked to take upon ourselves not only our own failures, but those of the Jewish people as a whole, it may be worthwhile, at least once a year, to picture ourselves as serial sinners in the hands of an exasperated God. We are awfully good, just like everyone else, at refusing to be ashamed. We find others who (after all) do worse, we think of ourselves just as victims, we come up with a clever argument when a heartsick cry would do.

Perhaps we should take our cue from the endearing but fallible Mr. Bennett in Jane Austen's *Pride and Prejudice*. I'm thinking of the scene not long after Mr. Bennett's silly daughter Lydia has been seduced by, and run off with, the evil Mr. Wickham. Our heroine, the wiser daughter Elizabeth, tries to console her father—and yet, writes Austen,

> ...on her briefly expressing her sorrow for what he must have endured, he replied, "Say nothing of that. Who would suffer but myself? It has been my own doing, and I ought to feel it."
>
> "You must not be too severe upon yourself," replied Elizabeth.
>
> "You may well warn me against such an evil. Human nature is so prone to fall into it! No, Lizzy, let me once in my life feel how much I have been to blame. I am not afraid of being overpowered by the impression. It will pass away soon enough."

Once a year, on a day of stern judgment, we too can bear to feel how much we have been to blame. We too can feel responsible for our collective foolishness, rashness, self-righteousness, self-deception, and the rest. We could have done better; we should have done better; we probably won't do much, in the coming year, very differently. So don't—the prayer interrupts us—don't let yourself either despair or make some promise to change. Instead, feel the *impulse* to promise, so open and eager. Feel the shame that it comes from, too. Now call to mind the twinborn senses of duty and sympathy that your shame roots down in: the standards against which you've weighed yourself and found yourself wanting.

That mix of emotions lies at the core of Kol Nidre as a text, as moving in its literary way as the famous Ashkenazi melody. It's not an easy mix to bear. It passes, soon enough.

CROSSCURRENTS

KAPLAN'S APPROACH TO PRAYER APPRECIATED AND CHALLENGED

Eric Caplan

Introduction

Mordecai M. Kaplan (1881–1983), the ideological founder of Reconstructionist Judaism, is an important figure in the development of American Jewish liturgy. Kaplan and his closest followers—Eugene Kohn and Ira Eisenstein among others—coedited the *New Haggadah* (1941), the *Sabbath Prayer Book* (1945), the *High Holiday Prayer Book* (1948), the *Festival Prayer Book* (1958), and the *Daily Prayer Book* (1963). Prior to the publication of these works, Kaplan oversaw the publication of two collections of readings to be used to enrich prayer services.

How can we account for Mordecai Kaplan's obvious interest in liturgy? The most common way of responding to this question is to point to Kaplan's famous desire for intellectual honesty in prayer. Kaplan believed that "In religion, as in everything else, we must not say what we do not mean."[1] Having concluded that it is no longer possible to believe, among other things, that the Bible was revealed, that God will send a personal messiah, and that the dead will be physically resurrected in the future, he could no longer pray the traditional liturgy and believed that many contemporary Jews were in a similar position. This explained, he thought, why so many stayed away from the synagogue. Kaplan's liturgical efforts were definitely motivated by his desire to put into congregants' hands a text that reflected modern belief and thereby made prayer more possible for them.

But the desire for intellectual honesty only partially explains Kaplan's liturgical efforts. It does not explain, for example, why over half of Kaplan's prayer books were devoted to supplementary readings, the majority of which do not serve as a counter voice to prayers that Kaplan found theologically troubling. It also does not provide any insight into why Kaplan was so concerned, in the first place, that Jews continue to pray. After all, he could have responded to the empty pews of his time by seeing the death of communal prayer as simply another stage in the natural evolution of Jewish practice. Sacrifices, too, were once an essential component of Jewish ritual life but ceased after the destruction of the Second Temple in 70CE. Not every component of Jewish tradition that dies needs to be revived. Mordecai Kaplan, however, could not stand idly by while Jews abandoned traditional prayer because he believed that prayer was essential to the realization of religion's primary purpose: motivating people to strive for a more just world order. And it is this belief in the importance of prayer that provides the most comprehensive explanation for Kaplan's liturgical creativity.

For Mordecai Kaplan, "The problem of serious-minded religionists is not: how can we get people to become religious? But, How can we get religion to make people better?"[2] Kaplan wanted religion to serve both as a catalyst for individual moral growth and for inspiring collective progress in the "struggle against poverty, disease, ignorance, oppression and war."[3] He recognized that achieving progress in these areas was not easy and believed that to persevere in the task an individual needed to have strong faith that the world and its people could indeed be perfected. Fostering that faith is an essential function of religion. It requires the cultivation in people of two complementary states of mind: appreciation of the world's blessings—for if the world already has good within it there is reason to believe that this good can be expanded—and the conviction that there exists a Force in the universe (God) that supports the human quest to achieve a better world and thus makes this goal attainable. As Kaplan explains,

> Every experience of success in overcoming the misery of cowardice, envy, hate and greed is an experience of God. Faith in God is faith in the possibility of such achievements, without which we inevitably sink into moral defeatism. That is why religious belief,

in the sense of faith in the Power that makes for salvation, is indispensable to modern man no less than it was to his forefathers, as reinforcement for ethical living.[4]

The purpose of prayer

For Kaplan, engaging in prayer is of great help in cultivating appreciation and faith in God. The Jewish prayer book (siddur) includes statements of thanksgiving. In the morning service, for example, congregants thank God for their souls, bodies, the natural world, the gift of Torah, and generally for "the miracles which are with us every day." The very act of praying in community engenders feelings of gratitude because humans are social animals who value and crave contact with others. Indeed, it is the experience of being in community that is partially responsible for our experience of God in prayer.

> The presence of the multitude in public worship creates an atmosphere that profoundly influences the individual participant. It stirs in him emotions of gratitude that he could not experience in isolation. He knows his life to be part of a larger life, a wave of an ocean of being. This is the first-hand experience of the larger life which is God.[5]

This quote makes clear how closely related thanksgiving and faith are in Kaplan's thought and how both of these are cultivated through prayer. The religious person sees life positively. Faith in God is the belief that there exists in the universe a Force that supports human strivings and thus insures that our positive posture toward life is not self-deception. Therefore, "When we are gratefully appreciative of the good in life, both the realized good and the hoped for good, we are experiencing the reality of God and communing with Him."[6] The more we sense the presence of this Force, the more we are convinced that the world can indeed be perfected. And hearing fellow congregants voice prayers that express the same values that we hold dear individually further strengthens this conviction. We are thereby reminded that we can rely on the cooperation of others as we strive to improve our world and ourselves.

Prayer as inspiration

Kaplan believed that the siddur in its traditional form did not articulate sufficiently all of the notions that had to be encountered in prayer if worship was to realize fully its potential for motivating the pursuit of social justice. He believed that the prayer book was unnecessarily repetitive, was too focused on petition considering that most moderns—including himself—no longer believed in a God who hears prayer or intervenes in history, and contained much "verbose adoration." There was a need to discuss more directly the difficult global and local realities that can undermine faith in personal and collective improvement, to augment the expressions of thanksgiving in the text, and to supplement the siddur's dream of a time when God establishes His reign of peace with calls for people to work actively toward the realization of this dream.[7] Because Kaplan believed that there were both religious and historical–communal reasons to continue to pray—with minor changes to the texts—selections from the traditional siddur, he relied heavily on supplementary readings to render synagogue services more effective.[8]

Accordingly, in Kaplan's Sabbath liturgy, for example, 60% of the book is devoted to supplementary readings. These include interpretive versions of inherited prayers, meditations prior to traditional rituals and prayers, interpretive psalms (cowritten with Ira Eisenstein), and antholo gies of biblical and rabbinic quotations (some of which are likely the work of Eugene Kohn).[9] The remainder of this article presents excerpts from these pieces. They provide a concrete picture of how Kaplan used supplementary readings to increase the likelihood that Jews who participate in communal prayer will attain that positive perspective on life that motivates individual and communal acts of *tikkun olam* (world betterment).

Prayer in response to adversity

Without a doubt, the persistence of both natural disasters, disease—especially ailments that strike people below the age of sixty—and the various manifestations of human-made evil, collectively serves to challenge the view that the world is good and likely to become even better. It is thus not surprising that many of the *Sabbath Prayer Book*'s readings address evil. For example, Kaplan inserted a meditation prior to the *Shema* affirming that

> The God of mankind is the God of nature. True, there is much in nature which endangers human life—floods, fire, wild beasts, diseases. But the more we discover of nature's laws, the more we learn how to make its powers minister to human needs. We therefore have faith that nothing in nature can defeat God's purpose of enabling mankind to achieve ever fuller, freer and more harmonious life.[10]

A similarly positive view of the natural world is articulated in Kaplan's interpretive version of the *Yotzer*, which asserts that "this world contains all that man needs for the achievement of his happiness, and puts at his service power beyond measure...All things in heaven and earth are (God's) servants...All of them offer help to man when he builds (God's) kingdom of righteousness."[11] Whereas it might seem at times that human welfare and nature are at odds, this is fundamentally not the case. By remembering our ability to harness the power of nature for our benefit and to use science to solve natural evil, we can counter the sense of despair that this form of evil can engender. We then realize that the cosmos does, indeed, support the human quest for improvement.

Many of the *Sabbath Prayer Book*'s supplementary pieces were written during the reign of Adolf Hitler. Suffering caused by dictators is therefore the category of human generated evil that is of greatest concern to Kaplan and his coeditors. Here, too, they see cause for maintaining an optimistic view of the world. Although God cannot intervene in history and eradicate evil, they assert that human history teaches that dictators cannot prevail. As they explain in the interpretive *Geulah*,

> Whenever a human tyrant usurps divine authority, and lords it over his fellow-men to their hurt, the hardening of his heart proves his own undoing; his overweening arrogance writes his doom. Therefore we will never be discouraged nor dismayed, when unrighteous powers rise up to destroy us.[12]

A similar thought is expressed in the reading, "God Reveals Himself as Redeemer."

> They who enslave their fellowmen, who exact endless toil and lawless tribute, who cheapen the worth of human life, and crush out its latent glories, are driven by their arrogance to self-avenging crime, and in their mad race for power, they plunge into the abyss.[13]

Kaplan did not wish the various manifestations of evil to cause people to despair of the world's essential goodness but he also did not want evil to be ignored. After all, recognizing the suffering that exists in our world is key to feeling the need to address it, and religion, as we have seen, must cultivate an activist stance. Accordingly, Kaplan reminds worshipers in the reading, "Life is what we make it," that

> The faith in life's goodness is not the complacency of the self-contented, of him who finds the world good, because he prospers in all he does. True faith does not avert its eyes from the want and the misery that mar man's world...Faint is the voice that bears gladsome tidings, small the measure of happiness in the world...– Despite that, Israel's faith refuses to pronounce the life of man beyond the reach of hope and betterment...It commands us to bring forth the best that resides in all things...This is true religion's call to repentance and redemption.[14]

Prayer as thanksgiving

The voicing of thanks for the pleasures of the world helps create a positive view of life by sensitizing us to the good that we already enjoy which, in turn, engenders confidence that more good can be obtained. This confidence is especially important when we face personal and communal crises. As Kaplan explains in *The Future of the American Jew*: "If, at the same time that we face the evil we fear, we are also aware of our resources, if we are inspired by a certain self-confidence and trust in God, based on past achievement...we do not encounter our problem in a defeatist mood, and our chances of success are immeasurably enhanced."[15]

It is thus not surprising that Kaplan chose to include in his siddur a number of readings that express or foster feelings of thanksgiving. Before the Friday night *Qiddush*, for example, Kaplan inserted a passage that calls on worshipers to use the Sabbath to cultivate a sense of appreciation. "Let us gratefully hallow the Sabbath by banishing care and anxiety from our hearts, and filling them with thanks for the immeasurable blessings that He has lavished upon us."[16] In a similar vein, meditations are provided within the Torah service to thank God for the joy of worship, the "wonderful and beautiful world" in which we have been placed, "dear ones whose love is our stay and treasure," and to voice the desire that God enable us to see the good of the world, "so that whatever our trials, we may still hold fast to our faith in Thee."[17] Indeed, because awareness and gratitude for the world's good is the foundation of seeing life positively, for Kaplan, the failure to see the beauty in life is a sin. A prayer is included in which the worshiper reflects with regret on a time when he or she "Saw only the shadows which now and again darken the way [and] forgot the sunbeams which so often illumine it...that the world in which Thou hast placed us is beautiful." It concludes with the hope that God "Pardon this my sin."[18]

Prayer as a call to action

Whereas expressions of thanksgiving and the faith in a Power that makes individual and communal betterment possible are indispensable to sustaining a socially engaged life, they do not, on their own, guarantee that a person will live that life. If worship is to realize its central goal—to "impel one to the service of man"[19]—it needs to be more forthright in its call for such service. The *Sabbath Prayer Book* includes a number of passages that do just that. The *Qabbalat Shabbat* service consists primarily of psalms that envision God establishing His rule over the world and ushering in a time of justice and peace. Kaplan prefaces these psalms with a meditation expressing the hope that reciting them will "fill us with joy and trustfulness and strengthen in us the purpose to hasten the coming of the Sabbath era of human history."[20] "Righteousness must be Lived," an interpretive version of the opening two chapters of the book of the prophet Habakkuk, speaks forcefully of the need to translate our lofty religious principles into concrete actions that make for a better world.

> Swearing allegiance to God and to His law cannot suffice; professing unswerving faith in the truth and the right is not enough.

Men must live their allegiance, and weave their faith into the pattern of all they strive for. Justice and love dare not remain mere iridescent dreams for the spirit to indulge in on Sabbaths and other solemn days. The Kingdom of God cannot be defended by those of mere passive faith, by those who are persuaded that God causes righteousness to triumph, regardless of what men do. Only that faith which impels us to live in mutual helpfulness can enable us to overcome the deadly enemies of God and man. God is a Lord of hosts. To be numbered among those hosts we must engage in unyielding struggle to make this world safe for all who want to be free and fair and kind.[21]

In the *Festival Prayer Book*, the Torah reading for the first day of Passover is prefaced with an editors' note asserting that the festival should not only be a celebration of Jewish freedom. Jews should use it to "deepen their understanding of freedom and work ceaselessly for the redemption of all mankind."[22]

Prayer as expression of universalism
Although Kaplan's desire that worship contribute to the realization of a more just world mostly impacted the supplementary readings included in the siddur, this desire also determined a few of the changes made to the wordings of the inherited Hebrew prayer texts. Primary among these is Kaplan's complete excising of all references to Jewish chosenness. Thus, for example, Kaplan's *Qiddush* for festivals speaks of God as having "brought us [the Jews] nigh to Thy service"[23] instead of the traditional assertion that God "has chosen and exalted us [the Jews] above all nations." From a theological perspective, Kaplan's God—the non-supernatural Power that makes for salvation—acts upon all people equally. This God cannot consciously select one group to serve a more important role in the world. To continue to refer to God as having done this would be a violation of the demand for forthrightness in prayer. And yet, Kaplan's approach to Jewish chosenness is more shaped by ethical–political concerns than theological ones.

For Kaplan, "Chosenness always means the superiority of the chosen over the rejected, from the viewpoint of the chooser" (i.e., God).[24] The idea that God would view one people more favorably than another is morally repugnant. Moreover, Kaplan believed that such views undermined religion's ability to contribute to the realization of world peace. This consideration is strongly evident in the *Future of the American Jew*, written in the immediate aftermath of World War Two. That war caused millions of deaths and great destruction. It was caused, in large part, by the German and Japanese perceptions of themselves as superior nations that should rule over "inferior" ones. With the creation of the atom bomb, such imperialist wars threaten to "destroy human civilization and, perhaps, the human race." To be relevant, religion must help humanity abandon the idea that one nation is better than another. "Unless [religions] play an important role in ushering in the one world which has become indispensable to mankind, they will be reduced to a state of obsolescence." But to make this contribution, religions must first rid themselves of the "imperialism" that lurks within them; they must give up all pretensions to being chosen, superior, or of having exclusive possession of the keys to salvation. Jews "must accordingly advocate the elimination from our liturgy of all references to the doctrine of Israel as the chosen people." Only when we have done so will we be able to demand of other religions that they make similar changes and thereby move humanity closer to a world where all people are viewed lovingly as brothers and sisters.[25]

Conclusion

The principle that public worship should inspire people to work to improve themselves and their world is clearly a worthy one. There is no doubt that encountering in prayer texts of the type that Kaplan included in his liturgies—expressing gratitude for the world's blessings, promoting faith that society can be improved by human action, calling for social justice work, addressing the challenges to faith posed by natural and human-made evil, and reminding us that other nations and religions share many of our core values and are of equal importance to us—can serve as a catalyst for acts of personal and collective growth. The traditional siddur only emphasizes the first of these five themes. Kaplan and his coeditors made a valuable contribution to Jewish liturgy by pointing out the need to focus worship on additional religious principles and concerns.

There is room to question, however, whether Kaplan's God has enough power to guarantee, as Kaplan asserts,[26] that the world can indeed be perfected. This is an essential point because part of the constructive power of prayer, in Kaplan's view, is that it reminds us of the existence of a Force in the universe that supports and insures the ultimate success—over time—of our efforts to improve society. For Kaplan, atheism's inability to make such a claim undermines its attempts to motivate social justice work. As he writes in the *Meaning of God*,

> No social idealism that does not reckon with the cosmos as divine is an adequate remedy. How can a social idealist ask men to deny themselves immediate satisfactions for the sake of a future good that they may never see in their lifetime, when he leaves them without any definite conviction that the universe will fulfill the hopes that have inspired their sacrifice, or is even able to fulfill them?[27]

As Mitchell Silver points out in his book, *A Plausible God*,[28] a comparison of the basic tenets of atheism and non-supernatural theologies, there is indeed enough good in the world to imagine that good is possible, but to insist that goodness will triumph is to overstep the boundaries of naturalism. For how can a non-supernatural Process guarantee the ultimate victory of goodness over evil? In the end, even Kaplan is forced to admit that this belief is rooted "in our need for faith in the possibility of achieving salvation, or the worthwhile life" and not in "demonstrable" fact. Accordingly, readings in Kaplan's liturgies that speak of the ultimate triumph of the good, while soothing, cannot be defended theologically.

Ultimately, if public worship is to foster social activism, it will have to move beyond the important calls for such behavior that Kaplan included in his siddurim. Week after week people encounter liturgies that express lofty goals and ideals yet the majority of us still do fairly little to address the social, political, economic, and environmental challenges that our cities and countries face. Our synagogues must become activist congregations and our services should include discussions aimed at evaluating our social justice work and committing to new collective projects. Only such services stand a real chance of attaining "the right spirit": the one that "impels (us) to the service of man."

Notes

1. Mordecai M. Kaplan, 1948, *The Future of the American Jew*, New York: Reconstructionist Press, p. 226.

2. Mordecai M. Kaplan, 1960, *The Greater Judaism in the Making*, New York: The Reconstructionist Press, p. 489.
3. *The Future of the American Jew*, p. 54.
4. Ibid., p. 202.
5. Mordecai M. Kaplan, 1937, *The Meaning of God in Modern Jewish Religion*, New York: The Reconstructionist Press, p. 249.
6. *The Future of the American Jew*, p. 304.
7. See, in this regard, Mordecai M. Kaplan, 1970, *The Religion of Ethical Nationhood*, New York: Macmillan, p. 54; Mordecai M. Kaplan, 1956, *Questions Jews Ask*, New York: The Reconstructionist Press, p. 461.
8. Kaplan also believed that the rabbi's sermon could contribute significantly to the effectiveness of synagogue services as motivators of social justice work. Sabbath services at Kaplan's congregation, The Society for the Advancement of Judaism, included a sixty-minute sermon (Ira Eisenstein, telephone interview, January 28, 1997).
9. It is often impossible to determine which of the editors wrote each of the supplementary readings. Whenever authorship can be established it will be noted in the footnotes. The ascription of the interpretive psalms to Eisenstein and Kaplan is based on Ira Eisenstein, 1986, *Reconstructing Judaism: an Autobiography*, New York: The Reconstructionist Press, p. 161.
10. Mordecai M. Kaplan, Eugene Kohn, Ira Eisenstein and Milton Steinberg, eds., 1945, *Sabbath Prayer Book*, New York: The Jewish Reconstructionist Foundation, p. 34.
11. Ibid., pp. 114–115. For Kaplan's belief that nature supports the human quest for growth, see *The Future of the American Jew*, p. 307.
12. *Sabbath Prayer Book*, pp. 39–40.
13. Ibid., p. 457. Ascribed to Kaplan in the footnotes to the book. A similar expression of faith in the inevitable downfall of tyrants is found in *The Meaning of God*, pp. 293–294.
14. *Sabbath Prayer Book*, pp. 426–27. Ascribed to Kaplan in the footnotes to the book.
15. *Future of the American Jew*, p. 305. It is thus not surprising that Kaplan includes "Thankfulness" in the book's discussion of the nine "Basic Values in Jewish Religion."
16. *Sabbath Prayer Book*, p. 56.
17. Ibid., pp. 176–179. All three meditations are taken from the *Prayer Book of the West London Synagogue*.
18. Ibid., pp. 251–253. This, too, is taken from the *Prayer Book of the West London Synagogue*.
19. Mordecai M. Kaplan, 2010, *Judaism as a Civilization*, Philadelphia: The Jewish Publication Society, p. 504.
20. *Sabbath Prayer Book*, p. 8.
21. Ibid., p. 431.
22. Mordecai M. Kaplan, Eugene Kohn, Jack J. Cohen, and Ludwig Nadelmann, eds., 1958, *Festival Prayer Book*, New York: The Jewish Reconstructionist Foundation, Inc., p. 161.
23. Ibid., p. 39.
24. *Questions Jews Ask*, p. 205.
25. *Future of the American Jew*, pp. 79, 153–154.
26. *Meaning of God*, p. 29.
27. Ibid.
28. Mitchell Silver, 2006, *A Plausible God*, New York: Fordham University Press.

CROSSCURRENTS

ON POETRY AND PRAYER

Rachel Barenblat

Yehuda Amichai is reported to have told an aspiring poet eager for advice that if that young poet could find fulfillment doing anything else, he should do that instead, and let poetry be his last resort. Poetry, said Amichai, should only be the vocation of those who can't bear to do anything else.

I've heard rabbis say the same thing—lovingly; ruefully—about the rabbinate. Poetry, say many poets—the rabbinate, agree many rabbis—is a difficult vocation. It has the capacity to be consuming, frustrating, and overwhelming. It will pull you away from your family. It will keep you awake at night. It may make you difficult to converse with at cocktail parties. For God's sake, if there is anything else you can imagine doing, do that! But if you can't imagine doing anything else, if the call to write poetry or to serve God is so strong that nothing else will do, then do it, and good luck.

I am amused by this confluence of conventional wisdoms because I am both a poet and a rabbi. When God was handing out vocations, apparently, I stood in line twice. And I should be clear about this: I love it. But it does pose some challenges, and people who know me in one of these roles are not always comfortable to discover the other.

Mention poetry in many religious circles, and people bring out treacly religious poetry which is drenched in sentimentality. Liam Rector, of blessed memory—the head of the MFA program at Bennington when I was a student there—would roll over in his grave if he could hear me attempting to find polite things to say about some of the religious verse

I've encountered. And I do need to be kind about these poems—at least, if they're shown to me by people I know. As a poet, I'm entitled to my critical and aesthetic opinion; as a rabbi, I need to respond graciously, and pastorally, to the vulnerability of the poet or the reader of poetry to whom this verse speaks.

But the tension cuts both ways. Mention religion in poetry circles, and many staunchly secularist poets will carefully back away. This distaste may stem from encounters with precisely the over-sweetened religious verse, which makes me wince too. But as a teacher of writing, I have long maintained that anyone and everyone can benefit by exercising their own literary voice—and as a rabbi, I feel certain that there is spiritual value for the pray-er in articulating gratitude or petition through the words of his own mouth, the meditations of her own heart.

There's a tension here: I encourage people to read the psalms and then try their hand at drafting their own, to read liturgy and then try crafting prayers which say what they need to say to God…but I don't necessarily want the results of these spiritual and creative exercises to be canonized. I try to walk the line between encouraging people to use poetry in their own personal prayer and replacing traditional liturgy entirely with personal or contemporary verse which would obscure or ignore the traditional *matbe'ah tefilah*, the flow and structure of classical Jewish prayer.

Given these contradictory impulses, and given poets' occasional discomfort with religion and religious people's occasional discomfort with poetry, the fact that I write (and pray) my own devotional poetry makes me exactly as popular as you might imagine.

Diaspora rabbis face the challenge of connecting congregants (and those who are unaffiliated but tiptoeing around the Jewish community's margins) with the depth and breadth of a Jewish liturgy, which is primarily written in a language those congregants do not speak.

Hebrew is a language rich with associations. Its structure of trilateral word-roots allows each word to carry subtle spiritual reflections of other, related words; as Rabbi Marcia Prager notes in *The Path of Blessing*, the word *baruch*, "blessed," hints at *berech*, "knee," as we bend the knee in worship; it also hints at *berech*, "fountain," leading to her creative translation of *baruch atah Adonai* as "A fountain of blessings are You…"

The poetry of Jewish liturgy is filled with these reflections and refractions and with the mental and spiritual hyperlinks that arise when a word or phrase from the Hebrew Scriptures recurs in a prayer. But most of the English translations in our siddurim don't capture these resonances. And translations that attempt to preserve the wordplay and allusions of the original Hebrew can be clunky. (I have a soft spot for Everett Fox's *Five Books of Moses* because of his attempt to capture Hebrew wordplay, but I know others who eschew the translation for precisely that reason.)

Beyond that, often the Hebrew originals depend on root metaphors which don't always speak to the modern understanding. And it can be difficult to convince someone who has rejected those metaphors that they are worth a closer look.

I am not a fan of pausing the worship service in order to offer intellectual explanations of liturgy. Stopping to explain the original context of the metaphor, or to try to illuminate the root metaphor in terms the modern worshipper might understand, breaks the flow of the service. It yanks worshippers out of prayer headspace and into a kind of classroom experience. (I love teaching about liturgy! But I don't think services are the time to do it.) I know that Hebrew liturgy contains words and ideas that are both important and relevant—but I'm not always sure I'm able to convey that knowledge to my community when we've gathered for prayer. Enter English-language poetry.

Probably, my favorite thing about *Kol HaNeshamah*, the Reconstructionist siddur, is the value it accords to contemporary English-language poetry. The poems in that siddur are, by and large, not poems that were written for the purpose of Jewish liturgical prayer, but they speak to some of the same themes as the Hebrew prayers that they accompany. Mary Oliver's "Morning Poem" ("Every morning the world is created...") adds new resonance to *p'sukei d'zimrah*, the celebratory poems and psalms of the morning liturgy. When they are read alongside each other, the texts enter into conversation. As a fan of both Mary Oliver and *p'sukei d'zimrah*, I enjoy taking them together from time to time.

Mishkan Tefilah, the Reform movement's recent prayerbook, also makes use of contemporary English verse—for instance, Adrienne Rich's "Prospective immigrants please note," although the poem's title notably does not appear on the page, presumably because without the title the poem is more universal. Other poems in MT were written with both spiritual and poetic priorities in mind, such as Rabbi Norman Hirsch's "Becoming," which begins "Once or twice in a lifetime/A man or woman may choose/A radical leaving, having heard/*Lech lecha*—go forth…"

When I'm leading congregational worship, I often leaven our services with contemporary English poetry. I think that the poems speak to worshippers in a way that prose may not. I hope that they open up some of the themes of the liturgy in new and meaningful ways. And sometimes the contemporary devotional poetry I share is my own.

In my own prayer life, my relationship with poetry-as-prayer has shifted over time. For a while, I experimented with assembling a liturgy comprised purely of English-language poems and praying those poems daily as one might pray the psalms. I enjoyed repurposing ostensibly secular poetry in this fashion, but *as prayer*, it only worked to a limited extent.

What I love most about poetry is also what I love most about liturgy: the attention we pay to language when the words we speak matter to us. A few years into my rabbinic school journey, I took the advice I'd received at Bennington from my advisor David Lehman and began trying to write contemporary Jewish psalms and prayers: poems that could double as prayer; prayers that could stand on their merits too as poems.

My teacher Reb Zalman Shachter-Shalomi writes in the introduction to his book *All Breathing Life Adores Your Name: At the Interface Between Poetry and Prayer* (Gaon Books, 2011) that his prayer-poems are "free verse evocations of themes and imagery inspired by our liturgy" rather than direct translations of the Hebrew prayers. I aspire to follow in his footsteps.

When I started out, I was thinking of the work primarily as poetry. One of my earliest prayer-poems arises out of the blessing recited in the daily liturgy which blesses God Who continually speaks creation into being:

BARUCH SHE'AMAR

Every sunrise and sunset, birth
and death, storm and flood, blossom
and snowfall. Every lip balm,

paperback novel, beggar and bowl
and hair salon. Every glass of water,
muddy gorge, mother
and market and corrugated roof.

Rhododendrons, dirty oil barrels
filled with groundnut paste,
filligreed teapots, emerald beetles,
scrolls, wooden tulips, bottles of beer.
Sequoias, crepemyrtle, dwarf birch.
Every rubber band. Every paperclip.
Every open sore and aching tooth.

How does Your mouth not tire
of speaking the world into being?
Almighty, Your creations cannot imagine
infinity without growing weary.
It's hard to remember
Your mouth is purely metaphor
though Your speech is real.

You speak every atom in the universe,
a mighty chord resonating.
Every fold of skin, every grain of sand,
every iceberg and hibiscus come from you.
If You ever chose silence, even for an instant,
we would blink out of existence
as though this experiment had never been.

I had fun imagining and revising the list at the poem's heart. I wanted the list to be surprising: dirty oil barrels filled with groundnut paste, beetles, and aching teeth are not generally the stuff of poetry or prayer. I was happy with the poem as a poem. But the first time I brought it to a service I was leading (I chanted it, using the melodic scale for the early part of the service on a weekday morning), I discovered that it didn't move easily through my mouth. I had read the poem aloud while I was writing and revising, of course—but prayer qua prayer turned out to require a different kind of sensitivity to the words and their music. To my chagrin, the part of the poem I liked best (the second stanza and its list) was the most difficult to pray.

In the years since I first offered my "Baruch She'amar" in weekday nusach, the poem has taken on a life of its own. In my Jewish Renewal rabbinic school community, several people asked for copies of the poem; it has since been read, or chanted, in weekday morning services in a variety of places around the country, including a morning service at the most recent ALEPH Kallah.

Perhaps in the context of a Jewish Renewal minyan, where chanting English words in nusach is not an unexpected innovation and where interpretive versions of classical prayers are appreciated as variations on a known theme, this poem works as prayer. But I myself do not pray the poem anymore. Writing it helped me fall deeper in love with the central themes of the classical prayer—that God every day speaks the world into being; that God is the One in Whose womb creation is nurtured—but these days, given the choice, I prefer to just daven the Hebrew.

Addressing poems to God has turned out to be a major part of my spiritual practice. Sometimes now there are days when I don tallit and tefillin, recite a few early-morning prayers, and then sit down at my computer and let my fingers hover over the keys until new words come forth. (Typing while wearing tefillin is challenging, but I find that the creak and pull of the leather straps helps keep me mindful of what I aim to be doing.) Here's the result of one of those early-morning sessions:

WITHOUT CEASING

The wash of dawn across the sky
reveals your signature.

Cicadas drone your praise
through the honey-slow afternoon.

The angular windmills on the ridge
recite your name with every turn.

And I, who can barely focus on breath
without drifting into story:

what can I say to you,
author of wisteria and sorrel,

you who shaped these soft hills
with glaciers' slow passage?

You fashioned me as a gong:
your presence reverberates.

Help me to open my lips
that I may sing your praise.

The third stanza was the first thing I wrote that morning. It had been in my mind since the previous night, when I had driven my feverish son through the hills of western Massachusetts and eastern New York in order to get him to fall asleep. It was *maariv*-time, and although I did not pray aloud as I drove (I had a sleeping toddler in the backseat), it seemed to me that the world around me was praying. I held on to the image of the prayer-wheel windmills until morning and wrote it down once that day's prayer-poetry practice began.

The ending of that poem plagued me. My first several attempts were too sentimental; as soon as I wrote them, I knew that they needed to be cut from the draft. It wasn't until the next time that I prayed the *amidah*, the central standing prayer at the heart of every Jewish service, that I realized that the poem needed to end with the prelude to the amidah, the couplet asking God to open our lips so that our mouths may declare God's praise.

Maybe the most ambitious of my efforts in this direction is a set of six poems written to serve as Hallel, the liturgical unit of six psalms (psalms 113–118) recited on festivals:

SIX POEMS OF PRAISE (HALLEL)

1. (113)
Yesterday's sleet has melted: I offer praise
the sky is a perfect eggshell: I offer praise

my husband has taken the baby out of the house
freeing me to wrap myself in rainbow silk

to squint into the sun and sing psalms
I offer praise

2. (114)
let all offer praise
to what brings us forth from constriction
when we remember to say thank you
the hills and horizon dance

3. (115)
You spun the heavens on Your unthinkable loom
and fashioned the elements of creation with Your deft hands

the heavens are Yours
but the earth is in our keeping

the dead can't praise, but we can
help us remember

4. (116)
I yearn to serve
as my ancestors yearned to serve

you have loosened
the cords around my heart

5. (117)
let every nation wake up, seized
by the yearning to praise

help us manifest mercy and truth
both are Yours

6. (118)
let gratitude well up like water
    lovingkindness is forever
let my community call forth
    lovingkindness is forever
let all who marry fear and awe call forth
    lovingkindness is forever

from the straits of depression I have called out
You answer me with heart wide as the fields

open Your gates for me
I yearn to enter and give thanks

help me know that what was rejected in me
is cornerstone for something new

this day, right here, was shaped by You
I want to rejoice in it

Dear One, bring us salvation
bring us Your help

You give us light; in return we imagine
festival processions, our arms full of branches

bless all who come in Your name
  lovingkindness is forever

There are references here which the reader familiar with Hallel might catch. In poem 1, I mention the joy of having the baby out of the house so that I can pray; in psalm 113, out of which that poem arises, there's a reference to God Who makes the barren woman into the joyful mother of children. The theme is there, but the nuance has shifted: yes, I am the joyful mother of children (*a* child, anyway), but I am also the mother who is joyful to have the personal space to actually pray for a change. The other poems in the series hint at the original Hebrew in similar ways.

    I think the poems work as prayer. I have prayed them, and I like their flow. But do they work as poems? That's the question with which I perennially struggle. I'm not certain that they do. As a personal variation on the psalms of Hallel, recited by a pray-er who can appreciate how these poems both reference and transform the original, these poems "work." But taken outside the context of that devotional recitation, I fear that the poems are merely derivative.

    Prayer requires a willingness to shed skepticism and to enter deeply into gratitude, praise, fear, petition, contrition, thanksgiving. This can be a stretch for we moderns who are accustomed to imagining, deep down, that we actually control our own lives. And this is not generally how secular readers approach poems. Relating to a poem purely on aesthetic merits is an intellectual activity, but prayer requires heart, not just mind.

Can a devotional poem serve both poetry (a master which requires precision, craft, and sometimes obliqueness and surprise) and the needs of an actual praying community? I hope that the answer is yes, but I'm aware that I'm not the best judge of whether my own devotional poems stand firmly on both their spiritual and their aesthetic merits.

Beyond that, there's something more than a little *chutzpah-dik* about placing my own contemporary creativity alongside the time-tested language of the siddur. The words we pray in the amidah are centuries old, the words of the psalms even older; I have no idea how or whether my work will stand up over the years to come.

I've come to think of these prayer-poems in terms of process, not just product. When I write them and when I revise them, I feel connected with something beyond myself: with God far above or God deep within, with the liturgists both known and unknown whose words make up the siddur I know and love. When I pray them, I reinforce and enliven that connection. Whether or not these poems become part of Jewish liturgy writ large, they're changing me. They're transformative work, not only in the sense of work that transforms an original text into something new, but in the sense of work that transforms its creator as it is made. For me, that's the deepest place of connection between poetry and prayer: both of them change me.

There are poems to which I return again and again, as I have done for years: Jane Kenyon's "Let Evening Come" and "Having it Out With Melancholy," Naomi Shihab Nye's "Jerusalem," and William Stafford's "You Reading This, Be Ready." When I read them now, I enter into the grooves which years of repetition have carved into my heart. I am linked, ineffably, with the many other times I have turned to these words. I know that in a year, or in ten, these poems will speak to me in still different ways.

The same is true in my relationship with the daily liturgy. As I wrote in my poem "Mobius (V'Zot ha-Brakha)," "each year the words are the same / but something in us is different[.]" (*70 faces*, Phoenicia Publishing, 2011.) The constant is the relationship that holds both my life and the texts. Both prayer and poetry reward one's willingness to be changed.

CROSSCURRENTS

POETRY AND PRAYER

Edward Feld

There are moments when we may be moved to spontaneous prayer. Those moments are usually times of tragedy or great joy when our hearts overflow. Abraham Joshua Heschel writes, "...Prayer is pleading with God to come out of the depths. 'Out of the depths I have called Thee, O Lord' (Psalm 130:1)."[1] But for most of us, those moments are rare.

A more common experience of prayer is our participation in ritualized prayer, confronting a prayer book that, though it is supposed to move us, can feel alien. Heschel, analyzing prayer, assumes that liturgical prayer, in the end, ought to lead us to the same inner expression as spontaneous prayer: "Words are like mountain peaks pointing to the unfathomable. Ascending their trails we arrive at prayer."[2] Prayer for Heschel is always an experience of depth, of ecstasy. But it is a mistake to approach liturgy expecting the same feelings evoked in spontaneous prayer—peak emotional moments—for liturgical prayer functions differently and, almost inevitably, if we think that the only meaningful prayer experience is one with the same depth, we will be disappointed.

The power of liturgical prayer is similar to the effect of reading a good poem. Indeed, most of Jewish liturgy is poetry. Acrostics abound, one frequently encounters alliteration and rhyme, and many lines follow a metric form; the text is nested in a variety of allusions: quotations of and plays on biblical words and phrases, as well as references to midrashic narratives and motifs and to Jewish ritual practice. But it is not only a question of form: there is a deep connection between the experience of a poem and liturgical prayer.

Poems are journeys. We are different at the end than at the beginning, although frequently we aren't quite sure how we got there, how the poem has worked its magic. The process is a slow unfolding, an increasing revelation, a studied removal of masks. If we skip down to the last line of the poem, we will miss the point. The time and work it takes to get there is the "message," the power of the poem.

From the end of the Middle Ages to today, Jewish prayer books influenced by the Kabbalah have in fact labeled the different parts of the service declaring their progressive development. The classification system is based on the Lurianic understanding of the stages of divine emanation: The service is represented as a progression from the most earthly to the most heavenly moments. The mystical and convoluted Lurianic theological system is not ours, but the idea of stages that it employs points to the way in which the liturgy does not rouse a single emotion but sparks a progression, a mixture of elements, a journey.

But we need not have a goal in mind. When we take a walk, we may have no place we're aiming to go—we're just out for a walk—in fact, we may have simply doubled back on ourselves, yet upon our return, we feel refreshed. In prayer, at times, we are conscious of our own thoughts, at other times, we are intent on understanding what it is we are reading, and at still other times, we may just be listening to the voice of the leader or the sounds in the congregation about us; Jewish prayer moves back and forth between study and internal reflection, between singing and silence, between listening and speaking. Indeed, many people might see prayer as a circling around a center rather than a steady progression—something which is true of many poems.

Apart from individuals who come to synagogue for an ancillary reason—say, guests at a lifecycle event like a bar mitzvah—most people who walk into synagogue have a vague but unarticulated sense of why they are there. These people who come to services know they want something to happen, but they are usually unable to articulate what they mean by that. They are there to find something—something they intuit that they need. When asked, they may respond that they are there out of habit, or because they think they are supposed to be, or out of a desire to be part of a community, but the unarticulated piece is that they still yearn for something more.

Like poetry, liturgical prayer expresses that which is experienced by the listener as pre-verbal. It captures a feeling we only barely knew we felt. The words are not ours. We know that we would never have written this text. Yet, something of ourselves has been captured here. We have found an opening for new self-understanding, although that fresh insight may remain unarticulated by us. We leave with an altered perspective, and at best, this new anchorage affords us an internal balance, a being at peace with ourselves. Were we to approach prayer as a set of propositions—I am praying for "x," I am asserting my belief that God is "y"—we would miss the point. We would be in the realm of philosophic propositions, rational discourse, or declarative disquisitions, not poetry. It is not that we have affirmed a series of truths, but that something of ourselves may have been brought to light.

For ritualized prayer to be able to do its work, we have to let go of the highly analytical, focused mind-set we maintain in the everyday world of scheduled work. Instead, we allow a certain music to transport us. I spoke earlier of the musical elements of poetry, rhythm, and verbal play—even intertextual allusion has a kind of musical quality. In letting go of a more everyday mode of focusing, we allow another perspective to arise. It is not that we give up rational judgment; rather in allowing another mode to dominate, we may experience a way of being in the world that yields a different sense of wholeness, a new sense of peace, a freshness with which we can re-enter the world.

Ultimately, our lives and the reality we experience are mysteries. Our own motives are mixed, never fully understood; the reality of the "others" we meet is only partially revealed to us. The world as it unfolds, even as it contains its regular parade of day and night, times of the year, and seasons of life, still greets us with surprise. A poem speaks to these mysteries. By delineating it, by shining a light on pieces of it, the sense of mystery becomes manageable, the realm of mystery is more defined and thus less dangerous, less chaotic. We speak of being "moved" by poetry. It is not only that the poem introduces feeling, plays on our musical sensibility, or that it may activate a different part of our brain than linear rational thinking does, but, in expressing its ideas in the way it does, it helps us to "awaken." Part of the journey of the prayer is to lead us to overcome the indefinable quality of un-ease which accompanied us to the synagogue. At its best, we leave the moment of prayer feeling connected, perhaps to the universe, perhaps to our neighbor, perhaps to the divine.

Poems depend on metaphors, and the relationship that is established through the metaphor focuses on some feature that suddenly makes us see things differently. When the poet compares a loud sound to the roar of the sea, we understand that that is not literally what he or she experienced, but the exaggerated comparison paradoxically allows us to see things clearly, it has opened a new realm of feeling within us. The best metaphors are not obvious, not clichéd, they may seem distant at first, strange, but it is this distance, this strangeness, which moves us to see things anew. The liturgy, like the poem, creates a mythological world—the world of the poet, after all, is not our everyday world—and having entered this poetic world, our own reality is brought into relief. The mythological world of prayer may be alien at first, but it allows us to see our universe from a new perspective—a moral universe that makes demands on us and moves within a teleological purpose. With this lens, we are able to focus on our obligations but also find assurance that we have a place in the world and that we are connected to a larger whole.

The gift of poetry is to hear another voice and so be assured that the world contains an other who may know the world as I do. Similarly, at best, we come away from prayer with a sense that we have experienced some connection with the world outside that goes beyond our limited self-reflection. It may be an awakening to a presence, an alertness to insight that is more than our own feelings, a gratefulness for the gift of participation in a larger whole—of having our song carried along with others, being able to see more than ourselves, of being able to see a whole world. When reading many poems, we may not know exactly why or how we have been affected, we may not even feel we fully understand the poem, but we know that something in the poem has spoken to us, a slender thread has twined from the heart of the poem to our own heart. We may leave the prayerful moment realizing that we have been touched in some subtle way. We would never describe the experience as ecstatic, but something mysterious has happened: a religious moment.

Notes
1. Abraham Joshua Heschel, *Moral Grandeur and Spiritual Audacity*, p. 257.
2. Ibid., p. 352.

CROSSCURRENTS

HUMAN RIGHTS NEED A HUMAN TRADITION

Gabriel Moran

Human rights language is the main currency of international ethics. Government officials everywhere praise human rights. It is a card that is difficult to trump. Despite criticisms of his administration for allowing the torture of prisoners, George W. Bush said in an interview: "No president has done more for human rights than I have."[1] At the conclusion of their 2010 meeting in Libya, the twenty-two Arab League members said that the need is "to support the principles of fraternity, tolerance, and respect for human values that emphasize human rights."[2] Were they aware of what this proposal might entail?

What everyone seems to agree upon might actually be empty rhetoric to avoid doing something about a problem. From the earliest uses of "human rights" there has been a danger that the phrase would be used as a political tool or else would refer to an unrealistic hope that morality could replace politics. Jacques Maritain, who headed a UNESCO survey of philosophers concerning human rights, concluded that "we agree upon the rights but on condition that no one asks us why."[3] That attitude is not adequate today. The need is to deepen and strengthen the idea while also acknowledging its limitations.

I have been teaching a course on human rights for the last dozen years. At least that is the way the director of the international education program at NYU always refers to the course. I usually call it the course on international ethics. I have never felt comfortable with the name of the course being human rights. While the advocacy of human rights or the preaching of human rights made sense to me, an academic course did not.

So as to avoid becoming a preacher in the classroom, my strategy was to approach the course mainly as history. But even the history of human rights left me with the feeling that there were some big unanswered questions about the nature and the very existence of human rights.

I finally got hold of my doubts about the history, nature, and practical value of human rights with help from a 2010 book by Samuel Moyn, *The Last Utopia: Human Rights in History*.[4] The book enabled me to identify my problem although it suggested to me a path to follow that is not the same as the author's. Moyn's provocative thesis is that a human rights movement did not begin until 1977, the first year of Jimmy Carter's presidency.[5] There had been scattered uses of the term "human rights" earlier in the twentieth century, and the idea was promulgated by the United Nations in 1948. The term "human rights" began to gain momentum in the late 1950s but it was not until the 1970s that "human rights" became commonly used both by readers of the daily newspaper and by lawyers, politicians, and international aid workers.

The United Nations document was called the Universal Declaration of Human Rights. Although it is now revered as a monumental achievement, it did not attract much attention at the time of its adoption.[6] One problem is its title in which the term "universal" seems to be misplaced. The Declaration itself was surely not universal; it received a stamp of approval by 48 nation-states (eight others abstained). Human rights literature tends to treat the Declaration as sacred scripture, which is a disservice to what the document accomplished. The writing and the approval of the Declaration were extraordinary achievements. Under the guidance of Eleanor Roosevelt, there were no negative votes; even the abstentions by the Soviet bloc were testimony to Roosevelt's skill and patience.

Unfortunately, the Declaration's focus was on a long list of supposed rights, an approach which undercut a realistic claim that a few rights are indispensable for every human being, that is, they are universal. The split between the United States and the Soviet Union was reflected in a dichotomy of political and economic rights; the split was already present in 1948 and became embodied in the two Covenants that followed in 1966. This disastrous dichotomy has outlasted the Soviet Union and obstructs thinking about *human* rights. In the United States human rights are generally identified with political rights; economic rights are assumed to be a "second generation" that follows.

Since 1948 it has often been said that "human rights" is just another name for what the eighteenth century called "natural rights." With that assumption the Universal Declaration of Human Rights has been treated as among the last words on human rights instead of an initial floating of the idea and the term. Beginning in the eighteenth century with Jeremy Bentham's description of natural rights as "nonsense on stilts," there have always been doubters and skeptics; Bentham insisted that real rights are the child of real laws. Natural rights that would be bestowed by a benevolent nature did not play much part in reform movements of the nineteenth century.

Some contemporary authors who assume that human rights are a renaming of the eighteenth-century's natural rights dismiss them. Alasdair MacIntyre writes of natural or human rights: "The truth is plain; there are no such rights, and belief in them is one with belief in witches and unicorns."[7] A more apt metaphor that MacIntyre could have used was belief in a fairy godmother. The Declaration of Independence refers to "nature and nature's god"; the Declaration of the Rights of Man and of the Citizen collapsed the difference between god and nature. Nature was the mother of us all. It is safe to say that human rights cannot be based on the eighteenth-century's attempt to retrieve a myth of mother nature.[8]

The term "rights" has been in common use since the seventeenth century and its beginnings go back at least until the twelfth century.[9] But even in 1971 when John Rawls published his major study of rights, *A Theory of Justice*, he had nothing to say about "human rights."[10] Neither did Ronald Dworkin in *Taking Rights Seriously*, published in 1976.[11] Moyn's explanation for why "human rights" emerged in the late 1970s is that it was a response to the failed political utopias of the 1960s. In this context, he calls the movement for human rights the "last utopia," a moral substitute for the failed political utopias. Over the last three decades, however, "human rights," according to Moyn, has acquired a political program that is at odds with its original meaning. If he is correct, "human rights" is built on a shaky and mostly negative premise. It would be the last utopia in the sense of the most recent but not the last in the sense of final because it is destined to be replaced by another utopian idea.

The story of human rights need not end with a seemingly pessimistic conclusion. Up until the present, the universality of human rights has been difficult to defend. Authors often do so by taking a so-called minimalist approach. In the United States that means securing "political" rights while leaving "economic" rights until later. A kind of minimalist approach is indeed the most realistic way to establish the validity of human rights. But minimum should refer to a few *human* rights that transcend a split between political and economic rights but are the basis of those other rights.

Henry Shue's *Basic Rights* showed how a minimalist approach could be effectively used.[12] His basic rights—physical security for one's person, the means of subsistence, and liberty of movement—are demands upon the human community. Governments have a duty not to interfere with these rights and also to work with non-governmental organizations to realize the exercise of these rights. The basic duty of the human community in its various embodiments is to care for each person in the relations that constitute his or her life. The idea of human rights is most tested by the beginning and by the end of life when it is apparent that each human being depends on the kindness and help of others.

The eighteenth-century's rights of man were an attempt to speak universally but in fact they only included adult white men. Human rights are not an extension of that meaning of "right" but its transformation. In contrast to Jeremy Bentham's statement that right is the child of law, human rights are rather the parent of law, the claim that a human being can make on the whole human race.[13] The voices of women as well as men, children as well as adults, the dying as well as the healthy, and Africans as well as Europeans have to be heard for the meaning of human in human rights.

Tradition and morality
My thesis is that only in the second half of the twentieth century did a "human tradition" take practical shape, and that just as political rights are embedded in a political tradition so also human rights have to be based on a human tradition. This human tradition obviously includes politics but it is not reducible to politics. "Tradition" is a problematic term, especially in the United States. From the beginning of the history that led up to the formation of the United States, "traditional" was suspect if not negative in meaning.[14] In the nineteenth century, "traditional" became the opposite of "progressive," and the country fervently

believes in progress. However, a consistent anti-traditionalism becomes itself a tradition.

The term "tradition" is of religious origin; it was a brilliant invention of the pharisaic reform in ancient Israel. Instead of attacking the priestly control and interpretation of the sacred texts, the Pharisees proposed that there was a second source of authority. In addition to written tablets given to Moses, there were oral truths that Moses received and have been passed down by word of mouth. The adjective oral would have been redundant as a modifier of tradition, at least until such time as the oral source was itself put into writing.

Inherent to the original meaning of tradition was room for debate as to whether the writing and the tradition were entirely separate sources or whether the tradition was the context for the meaning of the texts. A debate about the relation between biblical text and tradition has been present in the Christian religion from the beginning and continues today. Christianity itself has been interpreted either as a rejection of the Jewish tradition out of which it emerged or as a radical reformation of that tradition. The Christian Church incorporated the Hebrew texts into its own Bible while recasting the interpretation of their meaning. For interpretive keys to those texts the Church fathers could not get along without a claim to tradition, that is, a context for their "New Testament" writings.

The image captured in the term "tradition" is a "handing over." In a pre-literate culture, the idea of tradition could be said to encompass everything known from the past. The term "tradition," however, surfaced at that important transition when writing began to assert an authority over the past. In that light, the pharisaic invention of a second source can be seen as a conservative return to an authority before there were texts on which political and religious leaders based their power. The invention of tradition was thus a reassertion of a fullness of life that can never be captured in writing.

Plato feared that the spread of literacy would undermine human memory. The fear was justified because writing had such attractive qualities that it quickly took control of the memory of the race. Writing provides for accuracy, permanence, and wide dissemination of important human matters. Such was the power of writing that tradition itself came to be written down, although the whole tradition could never be captured that way.

Traditions could be put in writing and they were, but *tradition* retained its power as the context for all writings. Put another way, "tradition" is a verb, the act of handing on both written and unwritten material from the past; "traditions" is a noun referring to what is produced by and remains from the process of tradition. H.G. Gadamer, who has written extensively on tradition, states the paradox that "Tradition exists only as it becomes other than itself."[15]

The human race is in a constant process of reinterpreting the past or rather reinterpreting as much of the past that is remembered. History is a process of remembering and forgetting. Many people unfortunately have an image of history as a line that situates us between disappearing points called the past and points yet to come called the future. We are constantly encouraged to forget the past and look forward. Tradition is a resistance to that image, a reminder that the past is never wholly past and that the future is not here for the taking. Tradition's image is human practices that have drawn commentary and then commentary upon the commentary. Tradition piles up the past; any attempt to create a new world finds a stubborn obstacle in tradition. On the other hand, anyone who wishes to engage in a radical transformation of what exists will find tradition to be an indispensable source of content, inspiration, and helpful cautions.[16]

The modern temptation to think that time can be mastered by escaping the past and creating the future was best mocked in the twentieth-century plays of Samuel Beckett.

The character Winnie in *Happy Days* keeps singing of a bright future even as the ground comes up to meet her, covered to her waist in the first act, covered to her neck in the second. The character in *The Unnamable* points out that "time doesn't pass, don't pass from you, why it piles up all about you; instant on instant, on all sides, deeper and deeper, thicker and thicker….it buries you grain by grain…buried under the seconds, saying any old thing, your mouth full of sand." In *Endgame*, Clov asks Hamm: "Do you believe in the life to come?" Hamm answers: "Mine was always that… Moment upon moment, pattering down, like the millet grains . . . and all life long you wait for that to mount up to a life."[17]

The traditions that have been generated by tradition are not necessarily good. In fact, one has to expect that the content of tradition is a mixture of good and bad. Some developments have enriched the tradition and other developments have proved to be (or will prove to be) distortions. Only a wide and deep knowledge of the tradition enables someone to judge that an item is consistent or inconsistent with the whole tradition. "Everything figures by comparison not with what stands next to it but with the whole."[18]

Traditions often have a person or a group of people who are elected or appointed to play the role of watchdog for maintaining the integrity of the tradition. However, passionate debate within a tradition is not excluded. Alasdair MacIntyre notes that "traditions, when vital, embody continuities of conflict."[19] In that context, premature agreements are one of tradition's greatest dangers. The leader's task is to keep open a running debate. Many conflicts are between people who are superficially conservative and people who are deeply conservative. The person who is holding on to something "traditional" from the nineteenth century may be unaware that it is a distortion of a richer vein of the tradition from centuries previous.

The term "tradition" usually has at least a shadow of its religious origin but it has been adopted by many groups for tracing an historical set of beliefs and practices proper to the group. Thus, there is a British tradition, a medical tradition, a liberal tradition, a baseball tradition, a jazz tradition and innumerable other traditions. If you are in the tradition, you know things that are not written down and you engage in practices that are shaped by a history whether or not you consciously attend to that history. The way to be educated in a tradition is to practice it and gradually pick up the interpretation of the practices.

From the beginning of the race, there has been an inchoate human tradition but the richness of what the human includes has never been available. An ancient Chinese thinker, a Roman philosopher, or the author of the Book of Genesis could conceive of "humanity" but could not fill out the variety of beliefs and practices of people everywhere. Eighteenth-century philosophers did know more about human history but they were still very limited in their knowledge of all peoples everywhere. Today, we know a lot more but we must still remember our limits. If an ancient or early modern thinker could be shown the Internet, the reaction would probably be one of envy at the material so easily available, but also doubt that human wisdom is achieved by an avalanche of data that no human being can assimilate. Google cannot give shape to human history and human tradition.

Whether we are wiser than our predecessors is very doubtful. In the most "advanced" countries the split between the rich and the poor is obscenely large and has continued to worsen during the last few decades. At some point there has to be a major overhaul in how the world's goods are distributed. That revolution is needed before the rights that are human can be effectively recognized for all. Perhaps today's uprisings herald such a change but there is nothing inevitable about the success of revolutions.

Where progress of a sort has been made is that diverse parts of the human race now have a voice that was previously lacking to them. Not everyone gets heard, but there is now an opportunity to oppose the assumption that some human beings are less than human and therefore are not to be included in the idea of rights. Aristotle could hold the view that some human beings are born to be slaves; that view would not find much support today. Despite their reverence for the founding fathers, the Republicans who read the U.S Constitution on the House floor in January 2011 could not bring themselves to read Article I, section 2, paragraph 3, which counts a slave as three-fifths of a person.

The 1960s were a time of great upheaval that resonated worldwide. It is true that the idealistic hopes of political transformation in that decade failed to be realized. However, the decade was more about "cultural" change than politics and many of those changes have continued and gone further. Modern communication and travel, along with interlocking economic systems, unite the peoples of the world whether or not they are ready for it. Today's context for economic, environmental, social, and political questions is the human race in both its unity and diversity. People may be oblivious of this context but they regularly get reminders that a single killing, an offhand remark, or a damaged nuclear reactor in a distant part of the world can have reverberations in their own lives.

The idea of tradition is often assumed to be the obstacle to universality but it is actually the basis for movement toward universality. Alasdair MacIntyre has written extensively on the need to root moral judgments in a tradition. Chris Brown argues that "if it is the tradition itself that is the justification for a particular practice, the potential for universalist claims goes by the board, or at least is severely damaged."[20] But recognition that judgments of right and wrong vary according to society or culture need not lead to "moral relativism." The alternative possibility is one of global communication to find human commonality. The convergence of many traditions is the path to what at some point can be called human tradition.

Human rights, if they are to be effective, have to be seen as the moral grounding of politics, not an alternative to politics. Human rights are not a matter of choosing "values over interests," as some authors put it. Human rights have to be part of the discussion of what constitutes the genuine interests of persons, communities, and nations. That is why the political cannot be separated from the economic, cultural, and social, as if politics were an isolated area with its own rules apart from the rest of life. That is also why morality cannot be thought of as rules imposed on individual behavior but irrelevant for nation-states. The moral question is whether human behavior serves the good of persons, communities, and nations. Human rights, although few in number, have to be the support of the political, economic, cultural, and social life of the human community.

Religion and human rights

The term "tradition" can be used today for referring to diverse religions. One could say paradoxically that "tradition" is a more religious term than "religion." Although it is not practical to avoid "religion," the term has some built-in bias. In contrast, there is little opposition to referring to Jewish tradition, Buddhist tradition, or Confucian tradition.

Religion can be a source of the worst violations of human rights, and it can also be a chief inspiration for the basis and practice of human rights. Christian writers have sometimes claimed that human rights originated from Christian belief.[21] Today, some Muslim writers make the same claim for their religion.[22] The evidence is not persuasive in either case. Until very recently there was no discussion or advocacy of human rights in Christian, Muslim, or any other religion. Making claim to be the source of the idea undercuts the genuine contribution that each religious tradition can make.

Although no one religious tradition is the basis of human rights, a plurality of religious traditions has to be part of the human tradition to support human rights. The word "plurality" is meant to suggest not only the fact but also the legitimacy of many religions. "Religion" as meaning a multiplicity of institutions and traditions has been the case only since the late sixteenth century. Before that, "religion" was a set of practices, only one of which could be true religion.

Today, "religion" can refer to the many religions that exist as important human phenomena worthy of study. The literature on human rights tends to dismiss when it does not oppose religion. Advocates of violence in the name of God give a bad name to religion. But the correction of that problem includes allowing into the discussion the voices of thoughtful and responsible representatives of religious traditions. A compatibility with religious traditions is an indispensable minimum if human rights are to be accepted and practiced by hundreds of millions of ordinary people.

Until the twentieth century, members of one religion could live with little attention to other religions. Some traditions remained almost totally isolated from one another until the twentieth century. Dialogue between religions was not a priority. Doctrinal beliefs might be implicitly offensive to other religions but the beliefs were intended for intramural consumption. Modern forms of communication and travel have made that isolation increasingly difficult. The only choice today is for different religions to engage in peaceful conversations with each other or else for these religions to be the source of violent clashes. In particular, Christians and Muslims need mutual understanding if there is to be any peace in the world.

Dignity and human rights
The term "dignity" is closely associated with human rights. At his speech before the United Nations on September 22, 2010, President Barack Obama affirmed that "dignity is a human right." That is not the most helpful use of the word. Dignity can be better thought of as the premise of human rights. As is true of human rights, most people simply nod in approval at the term "dignity." The problem is that "dignity" has a more complicated history and ambiguous meaning than are usually recognized.

"Dignity" is a word of Latin origin. In Roman times it referred to the respect which a gentleman was due from the lower classes. Some people possessed dignity, while other people were forced to supply it. The slow movement toward a more democratic world was signaled by the spread of "dignity" to a wider population. In the Middle Ages mystics, such as Meister Eckhart, affirmed that every human being possesses dignity simply by the fact of being human. "Every man a nobleman" was one of Eckhart's sayings which was difficult to imagine as a political reality but expressive of Eckhart's insistence that all humans possess a greatness in their being creatures before an all powerful creator.[23]

"Dignity" made the leap from medieval language to the modern era but at a cost. The dignity of the human was identified with the individual's capacity to think rationally and act independently. This was not good news for any earthling that is not human and for human beings whose rationality and agency are severely limited. "Man" was said to have dignity; the only opponent was thought to be "nature" and "she" would eventually be conquered. The power that man was to have over nature turned out to be a power which some men had over other men (as well as women, children, and animals).[24] Despite some shaking up of the language of man and nature in the twentieth century, the idea of dignity is still widely assumed to be the individual's ability to control his (and now sometimes her) life.[25]

The inherent problem with the idea of dignity has always been that it seems to imply a servitude of some kind. An upper-class gentleman cannot exist without a lower class to serve, honor, and respect him. The spread of dignity to all of "mankind" still involved servitude, explicitly for the other animals, implicitly for women, children, and vulnerable people such as infants and the sick. Anyone who lacks independent agency is thought to lack dignity. It is not an accident of language, for example, that the phrase "dying with dignity" was coined to refer to suicide. One's last scrap of dignity, it is thought, is the right to kill oneself. In a hospice one hears a different use of "dying with dignity," as meaning the care that should be provided to a dying person.

These contrasting meanings of "dying with dignity" reveal the fundamental ambiguity in the meaning of dignity. Like a great many words, dignity has two almost opposite meanings. It can refer to something an individual possesses or it can refer to the respect due to someone. In a world of mutual relations, the two meanings can be seen as opposite ends of a single relation; that is, there is something proper to a person that generates respect in a community of persons. Someone who is doing the caring today might be the one who needs care tomorrow. But in a world of isolated individuals, dignity is up for grabs; those who have the power to demand respect will claim it for themselves. We need a comprehensive meaning of dignity that is based on personal integrity.

A violation of someone's dignity may involve interference with a person's "autonomy." But more fundamentally, it is treating an individual as something other than human. Torture not only causes pain but it is intended to humiliate the person by disrespecting the person's human integrity. The torture and humiliation of any human being is an attack on the idea of human dignity. Avishai Margalit in *A Decent Society* examines the ultimate basis of a "decent society" and concludes: "We have a simple formula which claims that a society is a decent one if it punishes its criminals—even the worst of them—without humiliating them."[26]

Steven Pinker, has an essay entitled "The Stupidity of Dignity." Pinker gives examples of what he thinks are "indignities"; these include a security search, a pelvic or rectal examination, and a colonoscopy. He concludes that since we agree to those things, "Dignity is a trivial value, well worth trading off for life, health and safety."[27] He entirely misses the point. A pelvic examination or a colonoscopy may be unpleasant but, far from violating human dignity, they express care by a competent physician for the person's bodily integrity. Pinker's one example that may be a genuine violation of a person's dignity—"putting a wand up your crotch"—is such a violation when the practice is no real protection of anyone's security and is performed with no regard for personal privacy. In any case, human dignity is not "a trivial value" and it is never worth "trading off."

An assumption that dignity is equivalent to rational control of oneself would make it impossible to cover all humans in human rights. In fact, the humans who are most in need of human rights are the first ones who are excluded. The literature of human rights almost never makes a reference to the environmental movement. That link is crucial for understanding that human rights are not asserted against the non-human environment but arise out of the human relation to all living beings. What is needed for human rights to be effective language is a dignity of all living beings, culminating in the dignity of the human being as "the workshop of all creation." The respect that dignity entails is a care that a person (or a non-human animal) should have its degree of independent activity affirmed while at the same time it is given whatever support and aid are needed for the enjoyment of its life.

Having a Latin origin, "dignity" is a biased term. What the Universal Declaration of Human Rights might have done was to explore terms in a variety of languages that converge in meaning with "dignity."[28] The idea of human tradition is still in the making and will never be finished. Still, the human race has reached some crucial stage of development. We are now members of one another in a way that was hardly imaginable only a few decades ago. A human tradition gained practical meaning only as an inclusive language emerged, one that includes dialogues between adults and children, Europeans and Asians, whites and blacks, women and men, gays and straights, rich and poor, Christians and Muslims, healthy and sick, artists and non-artists, and humans and non-humans. The reader is invited to add important dialogues that I have failed to list.

Notes

1. Interview with Ken Auletta in *The New Yorker*, January 19, 2004.
2. Quoted in Max Rodenbeck, "Volcano of Rage," in *New York Review*, March 24, 2011, 4.
3. Quoted in Mary Ann Glendon, *A World Made New: Eleanor Roosevelt and the Universal Declaration of Human Rights* (New York: Random House, 2001), 77.
4. Samuel Moyn, *The Last Utopia: Human Rights in History* (Cambridge: Harvard University Press, 2010).
5. Moyn offers such evidence as in 1977 the *New York Times* used "human rights" five times as often as it had in any previous year; Amnesty International increased its membership thirty times during the 1970s; a bibliography of literature on rights published in 1978 had only one book on human rights.
6. For example, in 1951 Hannah Arendt wrote a book, *The Origins of Totalitarianism* (New York: Harcourt, Brace, Jovanovich), in which she used the "rights of man," interchangeably with "human rights." The book does not have a reference to the Universal Declaration of Human Rights. A 1950 book edited by R.M. MacIver, *Great Expressions of Human Rights* (New York: Harper and Brothers) has almost no references to the UN Declaration until the last ten pages.
7. Alasdair MacIntryre, *After Virtue: A Study of Moral Theory* (Notre Dame, IN: University of Notre Dame Press, 1981), 69. The statement remains unchanged in the third edition published in 2007.
8. The two Declarations also draw upon a medieval meaning of "nature" as what a thing or a human being is. However, the dominant meaning of "nature" since the seventeenth century was nature as an object for human conquest. In this latter sense, natural rights were posited as opposed to nature. In short, the eighteenth century used "natural right" because that was the language it had inherited but the meaning of natural right by that time was a confused mess.
9. Brian Tierney, *The Idea of Natural Rights* (Grand Rapids, MI: Eerdmans, 1999). The term *jus naturale* before the twelfth century is appropriately translated as "natural law." In later

centuries, *jus naturale* can be translated either as "natural law" or "natural right" according to the context.

10. In later writing, Rawls adopted the language of human rights as an extension of the ideas of justice and rights that he had written about from the perspective of a particular society: "The Law of Peoples," in *On Human Rights,* ed. Stephen Shute and Susan Hurley (New York: Basic Books, 1993), 41-82.

11. Published by Harvard University Press.

12. Henry Shue, *Basic Rights, 2nd ed.* (Princeton, NJ: Princeton University Press, 1996).

13. Amartya Sen, *The Idea of Justice* (Cambridge: Harvard University Press, 2009), 363.

14. George Grant, *Lament for a Nation: The Defeat of Canadian Nationalism* (Toronto: McClelland and Stewart, 1965), 65: "The United States is the only society on earth that has no traditions from before the age of progress. Their 'right-wing' and 'left-wing' are just different species of liberalism."

15. H. G. Gadamer, *Truth and Method* (New York: Continuum, 1982), 241.

16. Charles Taylor, "Conditions of an Unforced Consensus on Human Rights," in *East Asian Challenge for Human Rights,* ed. Joanne Bauer and Daniel Bell (Cambridge: Cambridge University Press, 1999), 144.

17. Samuel Beckett, *Happy Days* (New York: Grove Press, 1994); *The Unnamable* (New York: Grove Press, 1978; *Endgame* (New York: Grove Press, 1958).

18. Michael Oakeshott, "Political Education," in *Rationalism in Politics and Other Essays* (New York: Barnes and Noble, 1962), 128.

19. MacIntyre, *After Virtue*, 222.

20. Chris Brown, "Universal Rights: a Critique," in *Human Rights in Global Politics,* ed. Tim Dunne and Nicholas Wheeler (Cambridge: Cambridge University Press, 1993), 109; Alasdair MacIntyre, *Whose Justice, Which Rationality?* (Notre Dame, IN: University of Notre Dame Press, 1989).

21. Jacques Maritain, who is quoted above as saying philosophers do not know the origin of human rights, was himself certain of the answer. He states in *The Rights of Man and Natural Law* (London: Geoffrey Bles, 1944), 45: "The consciousness of the rights of the person really has its origin in the conception of man and of natural law established by centuries of Christian philosophy."

22. Abul A'lā Mawdudi, *Human Rights in Islam* (Leicester: The Islamic Foundation, 1980).

23. Meister Eckhart, *Meister Eckhart: The Essential Sermons, Commentaries, Treaties and Defense* (New York: Paulist Press, 1981).

24. C. S. Lewis, *The Abolition of Man* (New York: Macmillan, 1947), 80.

25. An example is Michael Ignatieff's book, *Human Rights as Politics and Idolatry* (Princeton, NJ: Princeton University Press, 2001), 164: Ignatieff responds to criticism of his dismissal of dignity: "I now see…that you cannot do without the idea of dignity at all….While I concede this point, I still have difficulty about dignity….Dignity as agency is thus the most plural, the most open definition of the word I can think of."

26. Avishai Margalit, *The Decent Society* (Cambridge: Harvard University Press, 1998), 262.

27. Pinker, "The Stupidity of Dignity," *New Republic,* March 28, 2008, 30.

28. Kwame Anthony Appiah, "Response," in Michael Ignatieff, *Human Rights as Politics and Idolatry*, 106–07.

THEOLOGY AFTER OBAMA—WHAT DOES RACE HAVE TO DO WITH IT?

A Racial Prolegomenon to American Theological Production in the Twenty-first Century

James W. Perkinson

My concern in this essay is one of challenging North American Christianity concerning the ways our racialized history continues to influence and impede our national aspirations toward democracy and justice. In lifting up this concern, my focus is not primarily one of identifying strictly theological issues for strictly theological purposes, but one of making clear the degree to which race continues to dominate perception and broker behavior both inside and outside the church, even in supposedly "post-racial" America. In my short 60 years on the planet—moving broadly through church circles of all kinds—growing up Presbyterian, born-again evangelical at age 19, charismatic renewal "disciple" for decades, 15-year member of Episcopal Church of the Messiah on Detroit's near east side, Roman Catholic seminary trained, University of Chicago schooled, (not ordained) Disciples of Christ pastor/preacher for a year, poet-performer for 3 years for the downtown United Methodist Church in Motown—and simultaneously spending 9 years in the business world and another 15 years teaching for six different universities/colleges—I have yet to notice any generalized difference between Christian whites and secular whites in handling race. My concern then is not so much to tease out relevant theological themes as to outline racial meanings for theological consideration. In such a project, "God-talk" is secondary and after the fact. What first must be grasped is an underground tsunami of our time, only one of whose tributaries is conscious articulation. How the Spirit is moving inside of such remains a task of discernment possible only on the other side of plunging into the waters.

Framing the situation

In his recent book entitled *The Backlash*, *Philadelphia News* writer Will Bunch elaborates a tripartite rationale for the recent emergence of the Tea Party into the role of public adjudicator of political speech. Whatever actual electoral successes might ensue in coming elections, Bunch argues, Tea Party-ers have already proven potent in shifting public debate onto the terrain of right-wing concerns for "things American" by amalgamating rank-and-file conservative anger and panic with talk radio and social networking jingoism under the rule of vulture capitalism, "ever-circling" in search of popular means to further a big-business agenda (Bunch 2010). While reason three (big-capitalist "prescience" in funding rabid hucksterism and supporting Tea Party rancor) occupies much of Bunch's attention, the undercurrent of anger and fear that anchors the amalgam will command consideration here. Anti-racist activist Tim Wise has written extensively on the way the continuing subtext of race, in the United States, serves as an ever-looming portent useful for segmenting shared interests and organizing popular resentment into political sentiments and behavior actually at odds with popular interest (Wise 2010). The interest in this essay is precisely at the point where anxiety meets elocution.

It is no mystery that Obama's own party heads into a new election season laboring under an enthusiasm-deficit. Its own tacit covenant with corporate interest and mainstream mentality in securing electability required foreswearing strong shows of oppositional emotion. Obama as "icon of the new" could never step free from the deep shadow of our continuing struggle with race in this country. He remained intimately tethered to the great shibboleth of popular terror in the political imaginary: a public black man armed with both political power and historical anger. Gaining access to the top office of power required a clear and public repudiation of black indignation. As Wise has argued, Obama had to package himself as post-racially "pale" to have any chance of securing the mainstream support necessary to ascend the steps of the accurately named "White" House (Wise 2009). That pallor is the subject of this writing.

But as already indicated, the theological interest animating the text is one that works the intersection between word and energy, the place where palaver and passion intertwine to determine political destiny. In teasing out the argument that in many ways race today remains the most potent political fulcrum to manage "democracy" in service of what Citibank in a 2005 memo to investors called the newly emergent "plutonomy," I will focus on two moments of explicitly racialized public discourse with implicit theological significance that "bookend" the Obama ascendency. I will argue that the controversy around Jeremiah Wright during the primary campaign defined Obama's political currency in no uncertain terms. And the Andrew Breitbart attack on Shirley Sherrod in 2010 acted as exculpatory sanction for the Tea Party momentum organizing white rancor in utterly clear resolution to "take back the country" from its control by a racialized "other." The analysis here focuses on these two moments as metaphoric "iceberg tips," briefly exposing to sunlight the vast underbelly of cold whiteness that poses the true danger to the ship of state. Or said more prosaically, here in these two events the work of racial hegemony in manufacturing consent on top of inchoate longings and inarticulate angers that themselves remain implicit and intransigent becomes visible and revelatory. At issue in each, I contend, is the imprecatory force of the term "racism," as it has found employment largely in the direction of a "reverse" predication in recent public parlance.

Archetypal Obama

Before attending to such, however, it is worth tracking briefly, in phenomenological outline, the degree to which Obama is made to sum up politically useful "otherness" in contemporary political discourse. He becomes less a clear personality than a cipher and "place-holder" for agendas historic and resurgent. In keeping with the post-civil rights anxiety about blatant racial predication, color-blind racism today operates largely in terms of euphemism and code. As Detroit NAACP leader Horace Wheeler recently intoned in a conference in Motown grappling with the "Wright effect" on campaign fortunes, the landscape of significant racial reference today is organized under a triune bogey, simultaneously invoked and masked as "criminal," "illegal," and terroristic." That these terms today are explicit legal code for, respectively, "black," "Latino," and "Muslim" antagonists in the national morality play is patent, policing—figuratively and literally—"the other" within, at the border, and across the water. The slippage between each code and its reference is two-way and elusive, mobilizing racial stereotypes at unspoken or even unconscious levels of association, and in the same dazzling instant, reversing directions as innocent evocation or merely empirical comment. But it is also not recondite that each legal term mobilizes massive bureaucratic constituencies whose continuance in power is not separate from the "threats" those institutions are mandated to manage.

For instance, the steadily privatizing prison-industrial complex has mushroomed from an inmate populace of 300,000 in 1970 to a world-leading 2 million today—most of the increase coming from "criminalization" of inner-city youth on minor drug charges—while rural communities vie with one another to host prisons in their midst to increase employment prospects. Immigration and customs enforcement, working at cross and coordinated purposes with business interest in importing temporary labor on the cheap, catches the desperately disenfranchised victims of globalizing Latin American economies in a form of cross-border "whipsaw," whereby "illegal" status ensures incapacity to organize or otherwise seek legal redress from slave-labor work conditions and wages. And of course, Defense Department aggrandizement—as indeed defense industry profitability and the rampantly burgeoning private-contractor outsourcing—requires the prosecution of wars of either high or low intensity, against enemies "keefa-ed" or "burqua-ed" in "terroristic" mystery, to keep the U.S. population committed to military development and "green-zone" colonialism, as detailed, among many others, by the likes of a Chalmers Johnson (2004).

But criminalized "blackness," Latin "illegality," and a terroristically imagined Islam are not merely ad hoc racializations generated at the intersection of contemporary bureaucratic needs and popularized misinformation. They each have roots deep in the history of Euro-American relationships with others (the slave trade, the 1846 invasion and conquest of Mexico, and the *reconquista* of Spain from Islam only completed in 1492). Those political economy projects of racial othering were also theological projects structuring the deep text of whiteness in a long historical process whose transmutations are too complicated to trace here, but whose social undercurrents and explicit politics have never ceased to organize economic access, erotic imagination, or spiritual aspiration ever since.

Against just such a background, the currency of these tropes of race today is griping. Amazingly convenient is the degree to which Obama, in certain right-wing fantasy, has become the emblem of aspects of each. Under the "halo" of skin tone—despite half-white ancestry—he is unquestionably identified as "black" with all the easy slippage toward popular meanings of "African jungles" and "witch-doctor savagery" that association has never ceased to imply. In birth status—no matter the extant certificate—Obama is recurrently decried as outside the law in his claim to citizenship or eligibility for the Office. And by the name of Hussein, he is continuously cast as a Muslim "plant," poised to wreak serious havoc on our revered way of life. While not blatantly shouted down under any of the explicit code-terms, in Tea Party signs at rallies, the depictions are figuratively unmistakeable. Yes, he also is made to harbor hated meanings of highbrow elitism, anti-capitalistic socialism, and gun-control liberalism. But it is the racial undertow that energizes the tides of anger and focuses the force of the *ressentiment.*

It is no grand insight that times of economic disenfranchisement issue—almost invariably, it seems—in a ramped-up search for scapegoats. The reaction of course finds its archetype in Nazi Germany, but has been intricately theorized in ritual studies and the work on violence by René Girard, among others, and shows up in multiple theaters of action and exchange (Girard 1979). That popular angst in our time would find compelling focus in a central political incumbent, rather than a marginalized minority like Jews or "gypsies," is perhaps unique, though. But here it is imperative to keep in mind recent research unearthing the degree to which the centuries-long history of race in this land of the free and home of the brave has imbedded itself deep inside American brain chemistry.

Unconscious racism
Philip Goff, social psychiatrist at UCLA, for instance, offers evidence for the operation of a "racism without racists," joining other researchers in arguing that racial discrimination today is most insidious not among those who openly espouse their bias, but among the well-meaning majority who believe themselves free from prejudice, but nonetheless

continue to show preference for whites over blacks in hiring experiments where all other things are held equal (Bonilla-Silva 2006, Goff and Eberhardt 2005). John Dovidio weighs in with studies of "aversive racism," tracking the role of inchoate doubt in complex decision making, where the energies of aversion are deflected away from a conscious employment of racial criteria onto less invidious reasons for preference such as lack of experience (Dovidio and Gaertner 2004). Yet other research—duplicated *ad naseum* over recent decades—indicates more than half of whites have unconscious biases that lead to discriminatory behavior, and even that blacks harbor such—toward blacks! A National Opinion Center survey from the 1990s uncovers a belief in at least one negative stereotype ("laziness," "inferior intelligence," or "proneness to violence") about blacks among more than 50% of whites, while an Anti-Defamation League study puts the figure at 75% (ADL 1993, Bobo 2004, Smith 1991). In more informal association exercises performed at conferences, Tim Wise corroborates the evidence, but with a public admission rate to negative stereotyping on the part of whites that approaches the 90% mark (Wise 2008). And that is "admitted" activity.

But the most formidable evidence emerges in connection with Implicit Association Tests, correlating racialized imagery with rapidity of associative thinking (participants asked to link faces with positive or negative words), or other tests flashing images before participants at rates that cannot be consciously processed, coupled with magnetic resonance machines tracking brain response (Feagan 2006, Wise 2010). Here the rate of bias is above 90%. The magnetic resonance imaging testing focuses on amygdala responses of "fight or flight"—the same piece of brain anatomy responsible for PTSD flashbacks or aggression. While such testing also indicates that the first line of defensive response at unconscious levels of chemistry can be overcome if the imagery is slowed down to allow for involvement of the anterior cingulate cortex and the dorsolateral prefrontal cortex, the profile is patent. Racial bias toward blacks is ingrained in most white brains at the deepest levels of primitive response, as indeed black bias toward whites. But of course, the key difference here is recognition of which group has their hands on the levers of institutional power to translate such deep-seated antipathy into discriminatory action and social positioning that advantages their group at the expense of—indeed, *because* of—others. This is perhaps the most critical realization about race: that white advantage *depends upon* black (and brown and yellow and red) disadvantage.

The evidence of asymmetry is undeniable. A simple litany will have to suffice here for what is historically a complex and interconnected system. Two to three million cases of housing discrimination per year against people of color (McCoy and Vincent 2008). Discriminatory health care provided by the industry—according to its own studies (on top of the higher disease incidence rates across virtually every measure that reflect the life consequences of "racialized stress"—the duress of living under a racist domination structure) (Wise 2010). A job discrimination rate affecting 1.3 million people of color per year, involving 1/3 of all businesses and translating, in recent years, into an increasing number of race-based discrimination complaints (Blumrosen and Blumrosen 1999). A median household net worth disparity of 11 to 1 as of 2007—now closer to 20 to 1 given the disparate rate at which people of color were targeted by predatory sub-prime lenders and foreclosed in the "bust" of 2008—reflecting 33 years of federally promulgated racial red-lining followed by *de facto* segregation of the housing market (and thus stagnation of house values in neighborhoods of color leveraged by white avoidance of such areas) (CPR 2003). An educational system, disparately funded between inner city and suburban districts, regularly "tracking" disproportionate percentages of young people of color into remedial paths that usually end in low-wage service work, military "employment," or prison Lipman 2004). A criminal justice system functioning, as Michelle Alexander has recently demonstrated, as "the new Jim Crow," targeting young offenders of color with minor drug charges for plea-bargained sentences, thereafter stigmatizing such as a largely unemployable "caste" of expendables, ineligible for federal support in housing or education, vulnerable to garnishment proceedings to pay for the original incarceration time, left with recidivism as their only option (Alexander 2010). Within each bureaucratic complex of organization, the machinations of discrimination unfold in ever-finer grained modes of representation—re-arranging access, controlling opinion, constraining decision making, and reinforcing perception of racial stereotypes—in an almost irresistible machinery of social "prophecy" made to fulfill itself.

But all of this summation is background for the point to be elaborated here. Against such a generalized horizon of the purchase of racial perception on national life, Obama functions as a living lightning rod for the charged up content of the national psyche. As manufacturing continues to de-industrialize urban centers through automation and outsourcing, and finance capital finesses the Federal Reserve system into ever more exotic schemes of re-arranging public monies into private coffers (through the mortgage debacle, hedge fund backing of charter schools and privatized colleges, the marketing of credit card debt as the new "commodity" of choice, etc.), increasing numbers of middle- and working-class whites are facing starkly reduced expectations or dire situations of unemployment, bankruptcy, and foreclosure. The violated sense of relative entitlement finds its most provocative irritant in a chocolate President, who is also academic, liberal, authorial, and formal. But also useful for the likes of Koch brothers Charles and David and Rupert Murdoch, as Bunch lays bare.

As the new face of government spending and federal regulation, Obama's visage offers umbrage for all manner of elite bait and switch tactics. The bait is the skin tone and its historic associations—a classic hook into the racist panic stored in the amygdala treasury of things terrifying. The switch, of course, is the barrage of policy initiatives and/or details that further free big capital at the expense of mainstreet and the working class. Within this frame of reference, the Tea Party is perhaps nothing so much as a sacrificial bull, already angered by the pricks of economic loss and cultural threat, charging with intense focus at the wildly waving cape of Obama's face, unable to distinguish the real matadors from the falderal of a Glenn Beck or a Rush Limbaugh. But it is a spectacle offering a parable. The welding together of a simmering racial anger with a big-money policy-aim requires continuous maintenance in the theater of "common sense."

The elective affinity between popular anxiety over real economic loss and historic white rage is not simply a tautology. Again and again in the history of the country, the possible alliance between working-class whites and blacks around shared economic vulnerability has provoked elite class intervention. Whether in early forms of "motley solidarity" such as the "tri-cultural isolate" amalgam of slave "maroons" making common cause with Native Americans and disaffected whites (the Seminole Indians is perhaps the classic example), or the late 1880s coming together in the South of free blacks and poor whites in a Populist

Party initiative acting against planter class rule rooted in former slave plantations, or the growing melange of grass-roots activists of color articulating their anti-globalization struggles with small farming interests and labor unions in the Social Forum movement—social marginalization does not immediately and automatically translate into racial antipathy. The latter "achievement" requires public work, usually in the form of ritualized sanction. Certainly lynching contributed such in the Jim Crow South, soliciting and "resolving" poor white rage and middle-class angst in a climatic picnic atmosphere of collective *jouissance* that was simultaneously public pedagogy. In our contemporary atmosphere of popular dis-enfranchisement (and likely the beginning dissolution of the "American Empire"), I want to camp out before the "media-lynching" of Jeremiah Wright and "job-lynching" of Shirley Sherrod, to tease out the role of racialized communication in mobilizing generalized rancor in service of politics. More precisely, I want to suggest that alternative "white" media (talk radio combined with social networking amplification) effectively "conjured" black anger (Wright) and black laughter (the NAACP reception of Sherrod's narrative) onto the surface of the body politic at crucial junctures of our public process to "monkey-wrench" race in support of white hegemony and capitalist business-as-usual.

Wright's "Wrong"

In retrospect, the staging of Jeremiah Wright's half-decade-old sermons for national consumption in the midst of the 2008 Democratic primary campaign could be said to have constituted a rite of "white" initiation for Obama, demanding a painful public gymnastic of "passing" for a body too dark to accomplish such unaided. The sound-byte-send-ups ("God damn America!" "America took this land by terror from the Indians!" "America's chickens are coming home to roost!" etc.), circulated relentlessly like a religious white chant of "gotcha now, black man!" (directed at Obama's election bid) and attended by palpable glee among the white punditry, vilified not only Wright, and his south-side Chicago church, but an entire tradition of black preaching that cannot be dismissed merely as old school hyperbole. Drum-roll-like repetition of the clips' characterization as "hatred," "racism," and "anti-Americanism" sought simultaneously to open up the subject and close down any real examination of the issue. Arguably, this was not news as much as public liturgy.

I remember the daily routine for my Filipina wife and I, against our better lights, returning from teaching each day that spring, to sit fulminating and pained before the nightly spectacle (though our particular outrage was directed differently than what the screen ventriloquized). For months, the media fetishization of the long Democratic nomination process had churned up every least gesture and word—legitimately associated with the candidates or not—for daily drama and spicy titillation, like a postmodern bread and circuses routine, feigning ultimate consequence, trumpeting significance, demanding obeisance as if any other consideration of life must be laid at its altar of things important. So "lay" we did. And certainly the sudden advent of Wright's homiletic bombast was, at one level, not surprising. As already discussed, there are few hot buttons like race, in the American national psyche, to trigger instant vitriol and inebriating soliloquies of inanity! Keenly aware as our household is of the media as money-making machine, it was anything but astonishing that an ages-old talisman appeared, held up like a fetish-mask to draw out "evil" and exorcise its menace—all while increasing ratings dramatically! The icon of angry black man is immensely useful! Not surprising either was the fact that even though it was right-wing chanters of all things salacious that got the clip rolling in the first instance, it was the mainstream, so-called liberal-leaning voices who most vitriolically reiterated the unthought rant—again and again and again.

That a pastor's lifelong efforts to remedy south-side Chicago suffering and struggle could be served up like a burnt offering for national entertainment and entrainment, with nary a question of accurate representation or deeper investigation, for my wife and I, was a revelation not of Wright but of the country at large. America. Equally telling, for us, was the National Press Club grilling of Wright on the Monday morning (April 28) after his first public appearances (on Bill Moyers the Friday before and at a Detroit-hosted NAACP gathering the night before) since the video clips had begun circulating. The griller, as it turned out, had not ever heard the whole sermon in question—even though the Moyers interview had made it nationally available in that Friday telecast! (But then she was undoubtedly an exception. The rest of the punditry—and country—had listened carefully and weighed reasonably the content and cadence of the message in its congregational context—right?)

What was most overwhelming in those moments of watching was the seemingly unassailable triumph of sound byte vision that seemed to peer out through the typical talking-head eyeball like a national cult of spirit-possession. Its myth was freedom of thought. Its "reason" was the rapid-fire repetition of the latest epic assertion that America has ever been unassailably innocent. Its most trigger-happy emotion was the militant rage mobilized in a millisecond at any criticism of the nation. Wright's assertion of a patently central *evangelical* principle (that the God of the bible condemns—damns!—any violence visited on the vulnerable no matter who the perpetrator) was met with, among those commentators most "evangelically" persuaded, utter vilification (behind which stood death threats)! But in all the spin from all the liberal experts, much less the shrill Buchananesque voices, no other argument was heard than *ad hominem* attack. Wright's actual claim was never disputed.

Undoubtedly, that is because the history is as clear as it is relentless. America visited genocide on its native peoples, created its early wealth on the back of ruthless enslavement, killed half a million Filipinos in taking over its first colony, propped up dictators galore since the beginning of the twentieth century to secure corporate access to coerced labor and cheap resources throughout the Western Hemisphere (Nicaragua, Haiti, Guatemala, the Dominican Republic, Chile, El Salvador, Panama are only the most flagrant in a litany of intervention that scrolls like the credits after a blockbuster movie), cooperated with the World War I dividing up of the Middle East in the name of oil, used the helpless population of Grenada for target practice in preparation for Desert Storm, while the latter unfolded as a high-tech "drive-by" aimed at containing its own *hegemon,* Saddam, armed with the biological weapons supplied to him *by* us to face-down Iran *for* us, when he went rogue over oil in Kuwait and threatened the House of Saud, initiated sanctions for a decade knowingly consigning more than one-and-a-half million Iraqis to early graves (half of whom were children), before unleashing the latest version of "shock and awe" to funnel, one more time, U.S. tax dollars to U.S. corporations like Halliburton and Bechtel by way of a war zone, and continues to back illegal and UN-condemned Israeli occupation of Palestine at great cost to Semitic lives rendered "Arabic" and thus "expendable." This history of ruthless imperialism and rabid globalization never gets commentary or even denial because it is simply true. The media response is rather high-decibel vituperation of any such litany of fact as "extremist hatred"—never actual address of the reality.

But Wright was (and is) simply right—in both his precision and his passion. To merely list the massive damage would miss the meaning. Anger alone is adequate to the teeming—indeed incomprehensible—numbers of crushed bodies, dismembered children, widowed women, ravaged environments, bulldozed cultures and forests, and zombified populations reduced to living an incessant nightmare as menial labor for the global market. It is not that America is alone in occasioning these conditions for so many of the world's peoples—far from it. But it is unassailably true that America is no exception! It is also true that since the end of World War II, America holds the lion's share of both power and responsibility. That America has never fully looked itself in the eye and owned its own bloody hands is also indisputable—it has never had to!

But in the eye of a Jeremiah Wright—and a thousand other dark faces, preaching without flinching and refusing to mince the words—America has again and again been offered an opportunity to see. So far it has chosen rather to quarantine or kill than come to maturity. Malcolm X, Martin Luther King, Jr., any one of thousands upon thousands of quickly or slowly lynched bodies of dark resistance to the self-certain supremacy of white ways of naming things could have been the occasion for a cessation of denial and the hard but honorable work of national maturation. The quintessence of the humanizing "turnabout" (whether coded "religious" or "secular") that America has never yet ceased to avoid with a vengeance is confronting its founding "sin": the colossal hubris of using racial denigration to rationalize ongoing plunder. American middle-class lifestyle sits on a pile of commodities and garbage whose real economic condition is contraband, stolen at the point of gun. That we have more than 1000 bases or base-like installations in more than 150 countries around the globe is *not* for the sake of the well-being of others!

But woe be—literally damned!—the one who dares name such theologically in any public forum with the kind of acrobatic finesse and diss-rhyme duress of a Wright-like brilliance, such as he exhibited in the moment when on the spot before the Press Club. As he himself growled, in so many words, at the time—"they chose the wrong man to play this game with; I have been trained by a lifelong tradition of dozens-playing, from boyhood banter to adult rancor: where I come from, we do this for fun!" The combination of attitude and eloquence—face pontificating hilariously on top of the hard-hitting word-spitting—made the barb unbearable. "I'm unpatriotic? I spent 6 years in the military! How many years did Cheney serve!" It could not be dissimulated or side-stepped. It struck home. And, for this writer, that is exactly what white power needs in order to come to its own healing. . . if it would. . . if we would. And some of us indeed have begun. But the country at large insists rather on perpetuating its grandiose narcissism. It is uncanny how much the charges laid on Wright all along the way were so much projection. Racist hatred! Unpatriotic extremism! Egotism! Narcissism! If we (who are the majority) could actually set aside our terror at being discovered not to be innocent, and actually look at the clear history of our relations with the world's "others," we would find the pointing finger points at us. But I indeed dream. The chickens are coming, have come, home, no matter the volume of our histrionic "screedalism."

The real burden of my own white-faced lament here is in the word "lynching." Precisely such is what we witnessed in electronic form. It was promulgated by a postmodern posse using prime time privilege to round up the chosen darkie, hound him into a corner by means of insufferable lies, convene an instantaneous court of kangaroo opinion when he finally came out bellowing and strident in defense of honor and culture, then sit back in picnic-time glee when the more favored "negro" was coerced into kicking the stool out from under the roped-up body. Yes, it was virtual rather than physical. But the effect was the same: terror in the community. Watching the ritual "passage" of the would-be candidate in response, was agony. Obama's depressed demeanor and halt groping for almost unspeakable words of repudiation was enough to deflate an entire hurricane of hope in my household. And it served as utterly revelatory counterpoint to the "extreme-sports-like" joy irradiating CNN-MSNBC faces of pallor—a repudiation of the church daring to name the state in favor of the state silencing the church. The only thing more remarkable—and more telling—in the whole episode of outrageous white response to prophetic black anger was the by-line on the news that evening: "Obama *hammers* Wright!" The candidate did not have to exhibit even a thimbleful of the exaltation rampaging through white bellies to be credited nonetheless with "bombastic" defense of mainstream opinion. For the spin machine, the mere words themselves were enough to arch the toes in titillation! (And to enfold the possibility of change back inside the curtain of control.) White-shirted supremacy once again licking its lips over its latest stage production of black-on-black agony! It sure beat having to go rent *Birth of a Nation!*

But there is also a second thought here, a re-visiting of this debacle well after the fact. It is clear now in 2012 that Wright was not only pushed away from Obama, in what happened in the spring of 2008, but simultaneously brought near, and arguably left in the wings as a kind of shadow-cipher, "the other brother" in Civil Rights parlance (referring to Malcolm, if King's agenda be rejected), an offstage element of insurgent anger never far from the meaning of the pigment occupying the Office. Thus Glenn Beck could argue that under Obama policy (such as health care reform, of all things) is an ever-present specter of dark skin eager to gerrymander the policy in the direction of surreptitious reparations—and be believed by a significant percentage of the white population. This Obama-not-quite-removed-from-what-Wright-represents is then foil for a "take-back" agenda whose nostalgia runs from Reagan's "southern strategy," turning back the civil rights gains, to a Ron Paulesque reminiscence for unrestricted private sector practice, able to refuse anyone it wants in the process of doing business. How far back behind FDR this particular aim actually goes, among those like the Koch brothers or the Ruppert Murdocks, wielding their millions to fund the Party's parties, is not a pleasant suspicion to unfold.

Breitbart's bashing

Fast-forward 2 years to the emergence of a movement embodying broadly shared energies of disaffection that were given hyper-animation by the economic bust of 2008. The "R" word is once again being launched like a mortar across the political divide. The NAACP charges the Tea Party with tolerating racist elements in its ranks. Conservative blogger Andrew Breitbart tries to return fire by claiming the NAACP does the same thing among its own ranks. Is the firestorm that ensued to be understood as a clear "tit for tat," a moment of high-stakes "gotcha," demonstration that all groups are equally liable to being racist in a supposedly post-racial nation with a playing field presumed to be level? If we take Breitbart to heart—as if his floating of the video-cut was innocent and ignorant (!) of its context, as he quickly claimed in the aftermath (he who prides himself on paying attention to context)—what are we to grasp from the comparison he trumpeted?

The NAACP's July 13, 2010 call to the Tea Party to take responsibility for the racist imagery attending its own public outings cited rather unmistakeable expressions. Among its more egregious examples—signs of various kinds at Tea Party rallies styling Obama—sometimes in blackface paint-up—as monkey, as bone-through-the-nose-African, as "long-legged mack daddy," as Muslim; uses of the n-word on a sign and flung verbally toward black congressional members at a March rally; and Tea Party leader Mark Williams' blog, ventriloquizing NAACP President Ben Jealous in an Ebonics rant offered back through time to a supposedly racist President Lincoln, protesting having to work for a living and longing for a return to the "easy gig" of slavery.

Breitbart's evidence, on the other hand, was a two-minute clip, of a black Department of Agriculture official's talk at a recent NAACP event, evoking gentle and knowing laughter at the moment the official describes her own brief temptation to retaliate for the racial violence her family had suffered growing up in the South. The moment bears extended analysis.

In recalling her own journey from more than twenty years earlier, Shirley Sherrod recounts having moved from the deep pain of losing a father to white supremacist violence (whose perpetrators were never brought to justice), through a moment of temptation as a private advocacy firm employee in 1986 *not* to use her full powers to help a white farmer save his farm, to her present stance as an Obama official. Of course, the full forty-three minutes of the tape gives a remarkable account of transformation, of refusing to be locked into a retaliatory stance toward whites, of, in fact, deciding to fully help the farming couple in question (whose gratitude remains lively all the way up to the present, as demonstrated in their public defense of her actions once her firing became news), indeed, of a life dedicated, at no small risk or cost, to working for racial reconciliation for more than a quarter century.

But Breitbart's reiterated concern was not Sherrod's behavior as much as the NAACP's own response. In an interview early in that week, he described the audience reaction to Sherrod's moment of temptation as "clapping," but in later interviews amended that to a charge of "laughing," when no clapping could be detected at that point on the tape. Subsequent interviews with Breitbart did not offer anything else to illuminate the implied comparison, so what were we to make of the juxtaposition of this laughter and Tea Party sign-waving?

Despite having been hipped to the full import of the tape, Breitbart continued to claim that a knowing chuckle in such an audience, greeting a rich narrative of change, offered in a group of folks who have undoubtedly wrestled with their own experiences of racial discrimination and violence, having as its import the overcoming of any resulting hatred or retaliatory response in kind *remains the equivalent* of a sign casting a black official in some of the crudest white supremacist symbols of our national history, attended by grins or clenched-jaw glares, asserting not transformation but more of the same. Of course, each bit of communication—murmured laughter in the NAACP audience and sign-and-grin in the Tea Party rally—are mere tokens of something much deeper and more characteristic of their respective crowds, that does require context and narration to interpret.

The context is patent: a three-century-long history of *de facto* white affirmative action, accumulating some two trillion dollars of wealth on the backs of enslaved black labor, circulated largely among white families by way of inheritance and benefiting white communities by way of differential access to the infrastructure created (schools, jobs, houses, insurance, mortgages, police protection, health care, legal counsel, etc.), underwritten by the long tenure of overt white supremacy and more recently by a supposedly color-blind neutrality that nonetheless continues to maintain (and in some cases even increase) wide racial disparities across every one of the aforementioned social goods. It is also a context most recently generating (legitimate, I think) Tea Party anger at bailouts and big spending, which has also disproportionately targeted families black and brown with predatory subprime loans (and thus foreclosure rates) yielding the largest rearrangement of wealth in our nation's history—in no small part from communities lower-income and of color into bank accounts white and well-off. But I am missing Tea Party anger at this latter.

In such a context, Sherrod's full speech supplies the requisite (and remarkable) narrative and the crowd's response to the whole offers "call-response" testament to its reception. But the deep question is why the disparity? Why the difference in the first place and why the increase in certain cases? Boiled down to their basics, there are only two possible kinds of answers. Either black folks (or other racialized groups) "create" their own situation of disadvantage (through biological or cultural inferiority as evidenced in a failure of personal agency) or it is something that is foisted upon them by others who have more power to control the institutional practices and outcomes at issue. Either "they" do it to themselves or they are caught in structural dynamics nearly impossible to resist. Over the top of a basic conviction about one or the other of these two kinds of explanation swirl all manner of posturings and vitriol.

But anyone convinced of the influence of institutional dynamics is at immediate disadvantage in public debate conducted through two-minute tapes and sound bytes. Sussing out the impact of structural forces requires sophisticated statistical and cybernetic analyzes about exercises of power elaborated over time. Indeed, "racism" as a term was coined in attempt to move national debate in the 1960s beyond simplistic invocations of mutually held bigotries, and bring questions of power asymmetries and bureaucratic coercions into the picture. Obviously, that move failed, as "racism" today, for the average pontificator in our national screaming match scarcely means anything more than "personal prejudice."

Neither the typical news consumer (or pundit, for that matter) nor the passionate adherent of a party platform is likely to dig underneath the most immediately compelling image and snarl of outrage to try to gain some appreciation for how bureaucratic chains of influence work (tracking in grade school increasing the likelihood of dropping out in high-school increasing the likelihood of drug-employment as a youth increasing the likelihood of prison as an adult increasing the likelihood of . . .). Nor is there likely to be any recognition of the large-scale profits many links of the chain yield for various corporatized "players" positioned to capitalize on the resulting dilemmas (a political push for charter schools in poor communities yielding double-your-money investment returns through huge tax breaks and rents to Wall Street hedge funds; a gargantuan prison-industrial complex now the largest single employer in the country, yielding dividends to investors where incarceration has been privatized, and jobs to many rural white communities otherwise without economic prospect). That 70% of drug use in the country is by whites, while white incarceration on drug charges is only 10% of those jailed (and blacks and Latinos thus only 25% of users combined, but nearly 90% of those imprisoned for drug offenses) is of no moment for either the Breitbart crowd or mainstream media (CDCP 2006; SAMHSA 2003).

Large-scale social structural absurdities like these require way too much synthesis of complex processes for the average discussant. So our public debate rages on simplistically, continuously vulnerable to the loudest voice, the grimmest scowl, and the most penetrating augury of our historical storehouse of easy explanations. More blacks are in jail?—of course, everyone knows they are born criminal, or at least, born into a criminal environment! More whites have joined the billionaire club in recent years?—little question here why that is the case for the average white interlocutor (though of course, the vague certainty of entitlement based on a presumption of merit, rooted, ultimately in a taken-for-granted notion of Euro-American genetic and cultural superiority will not usually be explicitly invoked). And so the racial juggernaut rolls on, piling up ever more nuanced modes of translating racial stereotypes into economic advantage for those positioned to control the perceptions and anchor the practices in the national "common sense."

From this perspective, the term "racism" has not yet made it into our national vocabulary, except as a term already warped to reproduce what we think we already know. Its utility of revealing the way large-scale social structure encodes and perpetuates relationships of power, translating racial perception into economic advantage, has never been broadly realized. Thus Andrew Breitbart can float a two-minute video tracking titterings of laughter at an NAACP gathering, purporting that such a moment represented reverse racism. After all, Sherrod had institutional power over a white farmer!

But not only did Breitbart fail to do justice to the narrative of transformation and reconciliation actually offered, he in no way situated his claim in relationship to the broader outline of race in our day. The signs on the Tea Party rally portraying Obama as monkey have everything to do with the continuing history of disparities referenced in a statistic like a 20 to 1 net worth ratio between white and black families. How would NAACP laughter at the conference—even forgetting about context—"explain" that inequity? Blacks as a group are not, and never have been, in power over, or advantaged at the expense of, whites as a group in the history of this country. Quite the opposite—by indices large and small, all the way up to the present! Breitbart's attempt to mask such, by claiming blacks are as racist as whites, is a reprehensible effort at disinformation about the actual situation at hand. It can be construed as itself racist. It hides inequity under a disingenuous proclamation of equality, forcing one to conclude by inference that whatever actual inequity does exist could only be a consequence of personal failure. Which is precisely one of the ways racism reasons in order to legitimize its advantages!

Conclusion

But the real object of the Breitbart broadside was not actually white reasoning so much as white emotion. It worked the opposite side of the affective spectrum from the Wright send-up, but with no less potent consequence. Here it was laughter that was in the dock rather than anger—but the exhibition of the tittering had calculated effect. Whatever the outcome of the exchange between the dueling punditries, the chagrined and repentant politicos, the chastened activists, and the offended and ready-to-sue victim, the sound of many black tongues chuckling undoubtedly found a hearing in that already inflamed white amygdala. Where a Jeremiad of anger might augur terror and histrionics, tittering levity surely registered as indignation and a "how-dare-they" resolve to fight and be rid of the offending uppity-ness. That a black audience should find polite delight in a black woman wrestling with whether to get over on a white man, simply because for once, she *could*—what has the world come to?! Intolerable! Blink an eye, and *we* will be enslaved (after all, we did it to them, surely they will be just like us and want to return the favor)! Whether or not the charge of racism leveled by Breitbart could be made to stick did not matter in the least. What was of eminent political value was the spectacle of the soft laughter. It pricked the covert supremacy like a goad and loaded into it yet another image for offense. Between the wrong of Wright and the audacity of Sherrod, an entire river of churning outrage found the requisite channels to become a flood. How vast the inundation-to-come, and how in-discriminant the damage, now remains to be seen.

In the face of such, how shall mainstream theology speak? Will it continue its historic role as acolyte to the operative supremacy? Or will it take its cue from courageous figures (like Wright and Sherrod) offering prophetic clarity and long-term resolve, allow itself to be initiated into an alternative current of pain and beauty, and speak a new word?

Works Cited

Alexander, M., 2010, *The New Jim Crow: Mass Incarceration in the Age of Colorblindness*, New York: The New Press.

Anti-Defamation League, 1993, *Highlights from an Anti-Defamation League Survey on Racial Attitudes in America*, New York: ADL, pp. 8–25.

Blumrosen, A., Blumrosen, B., 1999, *The Reality of Intentional Job Discrimination in Metropolitan America: 1999*, New Brunswick, NJ: Rutgers.

Bobo, L., 2004, Inequalities that endure? Racial ideology, American politics, and the peculiar role of the social sciences, in M. Krysan, and A. Lewis, eds., *The Changing Terrain of Race and Ethnicity*, pp. 19–20. New York: Russell Sage Foundation.

Bonilla-Silva, E., 2006, *Racism Without Racists: Color-blind Racism and the Persistence Of Racial Inequality in the United States*, Lanham, MD: Rowman & Littlefield.

Bunch, W., 2010, *The Backlash: Right Wing Radicals, High-Def Hucksters, and Paranoid Politics in the Age of Obama*, New York: HarperCollins.

Centers for Disease Control and Prevention (CDCP), 2006, *Youth Risk Behavior Surveillance—United States, 2005. Surveillance Summaries*, Washington, DC: CDCP.

CPR, 2003, Current Population Reports, P70–88, Washington, DC: United States Census Bureau, pp. 2, 13–15.

Dovidio, J.F., Gaertner, S.L., 2004, Aversive racism, in M.P. Zaana, ed., *Advances in Experimental Social Psychology*, Vol. 36, San Diego, CA: Academic Press, pp. 1–51.

Feagan, J., 2006, *Systemic Racism*, New York: Routledge.

Girard, R., 1979, *Violence and the sacred*. Tr. P. Gregory, Baltimore: Johns Hopkins University Press.

Goff, P.A., Eberhardt, J.L., 2005, Seeing Race, in C.S. Crandall, and M. Schaller, eds., *Social Psychology of Prejudice: Historical and Contemporary Issues*. Seattle, WA: Lewinian Press, pp. 163–83.

Johnson, C., 2004, *The Sorrows of Empire: Militarism, Secrecy, and the End of the Republic*, New York: Metropolitan.

Lipman, L.P., 2004, *High Stakes Education: Inequality, Globalization, and Urban School Reform*, New York: Routledge.

McCoy, D.L., and Vincent, J.M., 2008, Housing and education: the inextricable link, in J.H. Carr, and N.K. Kutty, eds., *Segregation: The Rising Costs for America*. New York: Routledge, p. 28.

Smith, T.W., 1991, Ethnic Images, in *GSS Technical Report No. 19*, Chicago: NORC.

Substance Abuse, Mental Health Services Administration (SAMHSA), 2003, *Summary of Findings from the National Household Survey on Drug Abuse*. Office of Applied Studies. Department of Health and Human Services, Rockville, MD: SAMHSA.

Wise, T., 2008, ProtoTypical white denial. http://www.timwise.org, accessed April 2, 2008.

Wise, T., 2009, *Between Barack and a Hard Place: Racism and White Denial in the Age of Obama*, San Francisco: City Lights.

Wise, T., 2010, *Color Blind: The Rise of Post-Racial Politics and the Retreat from Racial Equity*, San Francisco: City Lights.

CROSSCURRENTS

WHAT KIND OF COUNTRY?
Economic Crisis, the Obama Presidency, the Politics of Loathing, and the Common Good

Gary Dorrien

The story of our time is that the common good has been getting hammered for 30 years. Wages have been flat for 35 years, and inequality has worsened dramatically. One percent of the American population controls nearly 40 percent of America's wealth and a bigger chunk of its politics. The crash of 2008 wiped out $8 trillion of home value, crushing the nest eggs of wage-earners. The banks that frothed up the crash are doing just fine. Much of the Republican Party is committed to delegitimizing Obama's presidency, and most of the Republican Party wants to bust public unions and break America's social contract with the poor and elderly.

All of this has created an opening for a democratic surge for social justice and equality. Mercifully, the Occupy Wall Street movement has made a start, but so far, the common good is still getting hammered, and Obama has spent most of his presidency cleaning up an economic disaster.

Throughout American history, Americans have debated about the kind of country they want to be. Today, America stands at the crossroads of a decision about the kind of country that America should be, which does not mean that a decision is necessarily imminent, since Americans are deeply polarized. According to the theory of "realignment" favored in political science textbooks, American politics decidedly "realigns" every 30 or 40 years in the wake of a breakthrough election. In 1800, Thomas Jefferson's Democratic-Republicans overturned the rule of the Federalists. In 1828, the Democratic-Republicans split into Democrats and Whigs. In 1860, Abraham Lincoln's Republicans pulled off the last third-party triumph, finishing off the Whigs. In 1896, William McKinley consolidated the Republicans as America's majority party. In 1932, Franklin Roosevelt's election paved the way to the New Deal. In 1980, Ronald Reagan's election paved the way to the capitalist blowout of the past generation.[1]

There is still time for 2008 to be transformational in the sense of these historic elections, ending an era of American politics. But time and opportunity are running out as the Reagan era endures in bizarre forms. Economic inequality, always steep in the United States, got much steeper after Reagan's policies took hold. In 1981, the top 1 percent of the U.S. population held 32 percent of the nation's wealth and took in 11 percent of its annual income. Today, these corresponding figures are 39 percent and 25 percent. The top 10 percent of the population hold more than 70 percent of the wealth. The bottom 50 percent hold 2 percent of the wealth. The share of America's income held by the top 1 percent has more than doubled since 1980, while the bottom 90 percent has, since 1975, coped with flat wages and mounting debt. [2]

For thirty years, we have had perplexed debates about how to account for this trend line in an advanced democracy. How could a nation possessing a strong tradition of middle-class democracy allow the middle class to be eviscerated? Economic globalization, to be sure, unleashed the predatory logic of capitalism, setting off a race to the bottom that feeds on inequality and obliterates cultural values and communities that get in the way. But globalization alone does not account for the American willingness to turn American society into a pyramid.

From the late 1940s to 1975, productivity and wages soared together in the United States, creating a middle-class society. Meanwhile, there were no bank crises, as New Deal reforms kept commercial banks out of the investment business. But wages flattened in the mid-1970s and have stayed that way ever since, while productivity kept soaring and commercial banks got deeply into the investment business. The rich got fantastically richer in the 1980s and 1990s, while everyone else fell behind, taking on debt to keep from drowning and to keep up appearances, as urged by the advertising industry. During this period, nearly every manufacturing-oriented society outperformed the United States in income growth and did so with more equitable distributions of income.[3]

Globalization heightened the necessity of using political power to defend the common good, but in the United States, the common good fell decidedly out of favor politically. The right to attain wealth was exalted over other values. The corporate race to low-tax and cheap-labor markets was rewarded with tax incentives. The religious, civic republican, and trade union communities of memory that historically kindled America's idea of a common good faded in American society, eclipsed by an ascending Christian Right holding very different social convictions. The American myths of Manifest Destiny and American exceptionalism were refurbished for political usage. Political campaigns became coded with racist images of black criminals and welfare queens. Liberals were redefined as guilty types that coddled criminals, imposed affirmative discrimination, and taxed working people to pay for welfare programs. Xenophobic slurs against immigrants were recycled from the least attractive chapters of American history. America passed three-strike laws and binged on prison expansion, filling its prisons with racial minorities. And social issues were shrewdly used to get working-class and middle-class voters to vote against their economic interests.

In the economic sphere, the consequences were devastating, fueling a surge for inequality. As late as 1963, the top bracket tax rate for individuals was 88 percent. From 1964 to 1981, it was 70 percent. Reagan cut it to 50 percent on his first pass and astoundingly got it down to 28 percent in 1988; he also slashed the top rate on capital gains from 49 percent to 20 percent and made it easier for the super-wealthy to pay most of their taxes at the capital gains rate. Policies favoring the financial industry and real estate over manufacturing and local communities were enacted, and corporations whittled their tax bills to nothing by exploiting loopholes and exemptions designed for them. The United States hollowed out its industrial base that paid decent wages, providing incentives to firms that made things to make them elsewhere. By the end of the 1980s, the top fifth of the population earned more than half the nation's income and held more than three-quarters of its wealth, while the bottom fifth received barely 4 percent of its income.

George H. W. Bush, after further exploding Reagan's debt, and Bill Clinton, succeeding Bush, restored some balance to the tax picture, which produced Clinton's budget surpluses of the late 1990s. But Wall Street fell in love with derivatives on Clinton's watch, with his help, and the financial sector began to gamble trillions of dollars on credit-default contracts. George W. Bush, succeeding Clinton, took no interest in regulating Wall Street's mania for extra yield, and his administration blew up the Clinton gains with tax cuts, two wars, a drug benefit.

By the end of the Bush administration, the inequality blowout of the 1980s looked modest, as did the Reagan recession. The chair of the Federal Reserve, on a Friday late in Bush's term, warned Congress that America might not have an economy by the succeeding Monday. That weekend, many Americans began to focus on whether they wanted to entrust John McCain with America's financial and economic meltdown.

Contrary to apologists for unleashed global capitalism and some of its radical critics, politics matters. Thomas Friedman, in his best-selling books on "turbo-capitalism," enthused that economic globalization—the integration of the national economy into the global economy through trade, direct foreign investment, short-term capital flows, and flows of labor and technology—has "flattened" the world. Global capitalism reduces national politics to minor tweaks, he contended. There is no third way in political economy anymore; there isn't even a second way. Any nation that wants a growing economy has to wear a one-size-fits-all "golden straightjacket" that unleashes the private sector, deregulates capital markets, minimizes government bureaucracy, eliminates tariffs on imported goods, privatizes state-owned industries and utilities, and allows direct foreign ownership and investment. Once a nation takes this path, Friedman claimed, there are no important political issues to debate. All that remain are "Pepsi or Coke" choices involving slight nuances of taste, policy, and local traditions. The "core golden rules" of the global economy have replaced most of what national politics used to be about.[4]

But the apologists for turbo-capitalism, which academics call "neo-liberalism," exaggerated the demise of national politics and the futility of attempts to channel economic forces. Neo-liberals were credulous about the self-correcting capacities of the market. They ignored that unionism and the NGO movement have globalizing capacities too and that governments were far from passé in this area before the global economy crashed. After the crash, governments stepped up dramatically, spending trillions of dollars to save capitalism from itself. Germany put up more than $700 billion, and Britain spent one-fifth of its national

GDP to save its banking systems. By March 2009, the governments of Europe, North America, and the leading Asian capitalist powers had spent or guaranteed over $11 trillion to save the system.

The neo-liberal boosters overlooked that governments played huge roles in setting up this system, defending and perpetuating it, deciding whether to regulate it, and dealing with its implications for equality, trade agreements, racial and gender justice, human rights and the rights of workers, immigration, and the environment. They played down the roles of the International Monetary Fund (IMF) and World Bank in enforcing neo-liberal doctrine. They thought it didn't matter that economic oligarchies in emerging and advanced economies entrenched themselves in national governments, rigging the game whenever possible.

Then came the crash of 2007, which played out dramatically a year later. The crisis that Obama inherited was thirty years in the making. Government was denigrated, and private wealth was prized over the public good. Speculators gamed the system, and regulators looked the other way. Mortgage brokers, bond bundlers, rating agencies, and corporate executives made fortunes selling bad mortgages, packaging them into securities, handing out inflated bond ratings, and putting the bonds on balance sheets. The chief rating agencies, Moody's and Standard & Poor's, instead of exposing financial risk, handed out triple-A ratings that stoked the lunacy, being paid by the very issuers of the bonds they rated.

So many plugged-in bankers, investors, brokers, and traders rode this financial lunacy for all it was worth, caught in the terribly real pressure of the market to produce constant short-term gains. Banks got leveraged up to 50-to-1 (Bear Stearns' ratio at the end) and kept piling on debt. In some cases, subprime mortgage bonds were actually created to allow investors, using credit-default swaps, to bet against them. There was so much money to be made that firms could not bear to leave it aside for competitors to grab.

Obama inherited a global deflationary spiral exacting portfolio contractions of thirty to forty percent and a free-falling economy that had nearly doubled its unemployment rate in one year. Deflation, once started, has a terrible tendency to feed on itself. Income falls in a recession, which makes debt harder to bear, which discourages investment, which depresses the economy further, which leads to more deflation.

Obama helped to break the spiral by coddling Wall Street and by pumping a trillion dollars of life support into the system. It worked well enough that eight months into his presidency, the fear of a depression had been forgotten and Wall Street was soaring. A year later, the nonpartisan Congressional Budget Office estimated that in the past quarter alone, the stimulus package had created or saved 3.3 million jobs and lowered the unemployment rate by 1.8 percent points. By then, it was clear that Democrats would pay a fearsome midterm electoral price for Obama's aggressiveness in saving the economy. Or at least, that was the reason that Republicans featured in explaining why the Obama Administration had been such a disaster.[5]

Many Americans are ideologically opposed to any politics that tries to rectify severe discrepancies in wealth, and the race to the bottom unleashed by economic globalization has convinced many people that nothing can be done about it. But both versions of this verdict are nonstarters for any moral perspective that maintains a connection to biblical teaching about wealth, poverty, and the good society. Moreover, the view that nothing can be done is untrue. If we think that we cannot do anything about economic disparities, we will soon be stampeded into believing that Social Security is unsustainable, Medicare and Medicaid should be gutted, and we might as well abolish what remains of the progressive tax system. Tellingly, American politics has reverted to debates about these very things, all rolled up with the politics of fear and loathing.

Imagining the hateful Obama

Obama is a lightning rod for the politics of fear and loathing. Millions of Americans did not dream up, by themselves, their convictions that Obama was born in Kenya, his teenaged mother forged an American birth certificate so he could run for president, he imbibed radical Socialism from a father he never knew, or his real father was an American Communist poet, he wrote *Dreams from My Father* to hoodwink prospective voters, or he got a 1960s revolutionary to write *Dreams from My Father* for him, he forged a political career by exploiting his friendships with Communists and anti-American activists, he sympathizes with radical Jihad, and/or his presidency is a conspiracy to inflict anti-colonial rage on America. There is a paranoid literature on these themes and a seemingly insatiable market for it. It is anchored in best-selling books, spewed in countless Right-wing Web sites, and legitimized with appearances and commentary on *Fox* television.

Jerome R. Corsi, a conspiracy theorist with a doctorate in political science from Harvard, is the king of this genre. Brad O'Leary, another early entrant, warned in *The Audacity of Deceit: Barack Obama's War on American Values* that Obama aims to destroy America's economy, bar Christianity from public life, legalize late-term abortion on demand, ban the use of firearms, and turn the U.S. Treasury into an ATM for the United Nations. Orly Taitz, the "queen of the birther movement," holds out against Obama's birth certificate and plugs for a conspiracy about Obama getting into Harvard as a foreign exchange student. Aaron Klein, a *Fox News* regular and columnist for the *Jewish Press,* updates Corsi's "radical connections" trope and adds birther material in *The Manchurian President: Barack Obama's Ties to Communists, Socialists, and Other Anti-American Extremists.* Jack Cashill, in *Deconstructing Obama,* contends that *Dreams from My Father* is a cunningly subversive stew authored by Bill Ayers that Obama is not smart enough to have written. Other titles in this burgeoning field include *Culture of Corruption: Obama and His Team of Tax Cheats, Crooks, and Cronies,* by Michelle Malkin; *The Post-American Presidency: The Obama Administration's War on America,* by Pamela Geller (with Robert Spencer); and *Obama: The Postmodern Coup,* a warmed-over Trilateral Commission conspiracy tale by Webster Griffon Tarpley.[6]

In the weeks leading up to the Democratic and Republican conventions of 2008, the nation's no. 1 best seller was Corsi's *The Obama Nation: Leftist Politics and the Cult of Personality,* which established the template for a gusher of anti-Obama alarmism. For Corsi, *The Obama Nation* was a campaign second coming, having made his early fame in 2004 by smearing John Kerry's military record as a Swift Boat commander in Vietnam. In Corsi's telling, Kerry was a fraud whose Silver Star and three Purple Hearts only appeared to top George W. Bush's military record. Corsi was an avid blogger for FreeRepublic.com, out of which his anti-Kerry book *Unfit for Command* was spawned with co-author John McNeill. The book rocketed to a number 1 best seller, but on its way up, McNeill claimed that he hadn't known that his long-time friend Corsi had showered the Right blogosphere with scurrilous opinions about Hillary Clinton, Islam, Muslims, Pope John Paul II, Kerry, and other targets of his bigotry. "HELLary," according to Corsi, was a "FAT HOG" who couldn't keep her husband satisfied because she was probably a "lesbo." Islam was "a worthless, dangerous Satanic religion." Muslims were "RAGHEADS" and "Boy-Bumpers." Muslims, Corsi wrote, were much like the pope in the latter regard: "Boy buggering in both Islam and Catholicism is okay with the Pope as long as it isn't reported by the liberal press." And "Commie Kerry" was "anti-Christian and anti-American," with suspicious connections to Jews.[7]

None of this disqualified Corsi from respectful treatment on Fox television or from attracting a prestige publisher for *The Obama Nation.* Corsi actually boosted his stature in 2007 by charging that President Bush secretly plotted to merge the United States with Canada and Mexico. In the fevered atmosphere of the far right, some dramatic explanation was needed for Bush's inexplicable "sympathy" for Mexicans. Corsi's book, *The Late Great USA,* offered an accusatory explanation lacking any evidence. The following year, he wrote *The Obama Nation* for a conservative imprint of Simon & Schuster directed by Mary Matalin, a confidante of the Bush family and former aide to Dick Cheney. In Corsi's telling, an Obama presidency "would be an *abomination*" because Obama is a lying, corrupt, anti-American Socialist and elitist who covered up his commitments to radical causes, plotting to subvert America with every waking breath.[8]

The Obama Nation pilloried Obama for employing a literary imagination and for taking literary license in telling his story. The Obama candidacy, Corsi argued, was nothing without Obama's story and the campaign's cult of personality, but Obama lied about his story, which made him untrustworthy. Obama's speech at Selma in 2007 laid Corsi's foundation. Speaking to a commemorative gathering at Brown Chapel a month after he launched his presidential candidacy, Obama set up a climactic rhetorical run by mistakenly asserting that President Kennedy financed the airlift that brought Obama's father to Hawaii: "This young man named Barack Obama got one of those tickets and came over to this country. And he met this woman whose great-great-great-great-grandfather had owned slaves, but she had a different idea, there's some good craziness going on, because they looked at each other and they decided that we know that in the world as it has been it might not be possible for us to get together and have a child. But something's stirring across the country because of what happened in Selma, Alabama, because some folks are willing to march across a bridge. So they got together and Barack Obama, Jr., was born. So don't tell me I don't have a claim on Selma, Alabama. Don't tell me I'm not coming home when I come home to Selma, Alabama. I'm here because somebody marched. I'm here because y'all sacrificed for me. I stand on the shoulders of giants."[9]

Corsi, not exactly prizing the feeling of the occasion, belabored the obvious literal impossibilities: Obama's father came to Hawaii in 1959; Kennedy took office in 1961; the Selma march occurred in March 1965, four years after Obama's birth; the Kennedy family had nothing to do with the first airlift of young Kenyans to America. Corsi saw nothing but lying, lying, lying in Obama's peroration, plus presumption at linking himself to Kennedy: "So Obama is again lying about history to claim JFK had anything to do with bringing his father to the United States to study." By the time that Corsi wrote his book, there was an ample literature in the Right blogosphere on this subject; often, critics added that Obama had never lived in Selma, either, so he was lying again. But Obama's spiel was a romanticized riff on heroic continuity and "some good craziness going on." To his audience of Civil Rights movement veterans, it was a variation on a stock biblical trope, "so great a cloud of witnesses" (Hebrews 12:1), where chronology was not the point. As for his bit about the Kennedy family, Obama confused the first airlift with the second one, which the Kennedys did finance.[10]

Obama's rhetorical shape-shifting at Selma established his debased moral character for Corsi, who piled on for 300 pages. Repeatedly, he complained that Obama's memoir refigured characters as composites and dispensed with chronology when it served his literary purpose, exactly as Obama explained in the introduction. He blasted Obama for withholding key information until late in the book, never mind that the whole point was to tell the story of how Obama learned it. The artistry meant nothing to Corsi, who saw only holes, deceit, and distraction. He demanded a memoir that enumerated the faults of Obama's father and mother from the outset, so that readers could feel superior to them and know where this story was going.

Corsi seized on Obama's remembrance, during his pre-adolescence in Indonesia, of being stunned by a *Life* magazine picture of a black man "who tried to peel off his skin." In Obama's telling, this experience "was violent for me, an ambush attack," one that conveyed to him that his race was a problem. Reporters found no such issue of *Life* or any other magazine picture of the time, and Obama suggested that perhaps it was an advertisement for skin bleaching agents that had wounded him. That was plausible, as skin bleaches have been marketed to African-Americans since the 1850s. The incident occurred to Obama when he was eight or nine years old; he was in his early 30s when he wrote about it; and he was 47 when reporters queried him about it. Obama acknowledged that the magazine part of the story was less vivid for him than the hurt it produced. Corsi knew better, declaring that Obama had lied again; it was only a question of determining the type of lie. Either Obama was a hypothetical liar who imagined an invented memory so forcefully that it became real for him, or he made up the story as a vehicle for delivering a guilt-mongering point straight out of Frantz Fanon's chapter on "The Fact of Blackness" in *Black Skin, White Masks*. The second option seems worse to Corsi's fans in the Right blogosphere, so they usually opt for it.[11]

Corsi could see no reason why Obama might have felt any racial angst while growing up in Hawaii; thus, nearly everything that Obama said on this topic fell into the category of "liar" or doubtful, except for the Frank Marshall Davis factor. Corsi judged that Davis probably did encourage Obama to think of himself as a victim of racial injustice. That would explain how Obama came to admire Malcolm X, came to believe his own childish fantasy about a black man ripping off his skin, and dwelt on Fanon's fantasy about a serum that turned black skin white. In any case, Corsi stressed, Davis was the first of many anti-American radicals that Obama befriended over the years.[12]

Corsi had long chapters of guilt-by-association on the latter theme, establishing the baseline for wilder speculation. Saul Alinsky, Jerry Kellman, Bill Ayers, Bernadine Dohrn, Jeremiah Wright, and Rashid Khalidi were the key players. In Corsi's account, Obama perfected Alinsky-style radicalism by working for Kellman. Ayers and Dorhn, the Weather Underground revolutionaries of the 1960s who got respectable later on, were neighbors and acquaintances of Obama's in Chicago. Obama absorbed black liberation theology from Wright; and Obama was influenced by Columbia University professor Khalidi's pro-Palestinianism.

In much of this discussion, Corsi explicated his material more objectively than was often the case with his successors, stopping short of wild theories about Obama's foreign birth or Davis being his real father. On the other hand, Corsi enabled some of the worst anti-Obama material by roughing up Michelle Obama, describing her as "the Angry Obama" who scared ordinary Americans. Michelle Obama did not come as naturally to elitism as her husband, Corsi allowed. However, she spouted snotty howlers about not being proud of her country until her husband ran for president, and during her years at Princeton, "she indulged in the luxury of experiencing alienation, instead of being grateful for the opportunity." Corsi shuddered at picturing the arrogant, radical and ungrateful Obamas in the White House, although he admonished readers not to say that Obama's Christianity was a fraud or that he was secretly a Muslim. Charges on these topics already filled the Right blogosphere when Corsi wrote *The Obama Nation.* Having come a bit late to the birther movement, Corsi did not troll in this area in his first Obama book; later, he compensated with a best seller titled *Where's the Birth Certificate?: The Case that Barack Obama Is Not Eligible to Be President.* This book's moment of glory was brief, zooming to no. 1 on Amazon's best seller list before it was released in April 2011, the same week that Obama unveiled his birth certificate.[13]

Although the wild stuff about outward conspiracies sells at high volume, its reliance on outward claims makes it subject to refutation. Donald Trump, after losing the birther issue, tried to switch to a race-baiting campaign centered on Obama's admission to Columbia and Harvard, but Trump's polls plummeted and he spared Americans of a spectacle presidential campaign. The best conspiracy argument, it turned out, operates differently. It has all the usual Right-wing charges about Obama's ostensible radicalism and otherness, but it works from the inside-out as a claim about his alienated psyche. Dinesh D'Souza, a popular conservative writer and former Reagan staffer, ventured into this area with typical boldness. A Dartmouth graduate and native of Mumbai, India, D'Souza grew up as part of India's first post-colonial generation, and in his telling, he has a keener ear for Obama's post-colonial animus than do other conservatives.

Corsi caught some of it, arguing that "Obama's black rage" is closer to Fanon's post-colonial experience than to the urban African-American experience of racial discrimination, housing segregation, and economic inequality. Obama seethes with racial resentment, Corsi assured, but not because he has ever experienced deprivation or oppression. Obama's racial crisis during his youth was a Fanon-like crisis of racial identity; it was primarily about wearing a white mask in a world owned by whites. But Corsi did not develop this insight, partly because he believed that Obama fabricated most of his racial angst anyway. To the extent that Obama had a racial crisis, it was a struggle for a self-determined racial identity, but *Dreams from My Father* was filled with lies, so Corsi put it aside, focusing on Obama's attraction to white radicals and Jeremiah Wright. *The Obama Nation* offered up a familiar stew of categories and accusations.[14]

D'Souza goes whole hog for the post-colonial thesis. In September 2010, he got the cover of *Forbes* magazine for a stunning piece of race-baiting titled "How Obama Thinks." The usual Right-wing interpretations of Obama, D'Souza urged, are inadequate, not wrong. To fit Obama into some strand or tradition of American history is to misunderstand him, for Obama does not relate to American history. Obama's vision has nothing to do with the dream of the American founders for a new order of the ages; it has no real affinity with the Civil Rights Movement; and it is not even best understood as a species of Euro-American Socialism. The key to Obama is African anti-colonial rage. D'Souza explained that Obama is a seething anti-colonialist dedicated to avenging the defeat of his father: "Incredibly, the U.S. is being ruled according to the dreams of a Luo tribesman of the 1950s. This philandering, inebriated African socialist, who raged against the world for denying him the realization of his anti-colonial ambitions, is now setting the nation's agenda through the reincarnation of his dreams in his son."[15]

This article electrified the sector of the Right that longed for a better account of Obama's obvious illegitimacy as an American leader. Rush Limbaugh, Glenn Beck, and Newt Gingrich heaped praise on D'Souza's brilliant insight and courageous truth-telling, which helped the book version skyrocket to no. 4 on the best seller list in its first week. *The Roots of Obama's Rage* repeatedly admonishes that Obama's father was a raging, radical, drunken, philandering Black Man from Africa. It claims that Obama's positions are too radical and bizarre to make sense as any kind of American progressivism. And it disclaims any personal animosity.

D'Souza explains that he is darker-skinned than Obama, but not black, unlike Obama, and that he liked Obama's 2004 Democratic convention speech. There are two Obamas, D'Souza says. "Obama I" is a sunny healer and unifier who wowed the 2004 convention with a speech resounding with conservative themes. "Obama II," however, is arrogant, controlling, and vengeful: "This is the Obama who lambasts the banks and investment houses and forces them to succumb to federal control; the Obama who gives it to the pharmaceutical and the health insurance companies, bending them to his will; the Obama who demonizes his predecessor and his opponents, portraying them as the source of all the problems that only he can solve."[16]

With so much arrogance at play, D'Souza explains, plus will-to-power and vengefulness, it makes sense that Obama supports environmental regulations, wants the rich pay higher taxes, and plans to withdraw American troops from Iraq and Afghanistan. But D'Souza cautions that the usual Right complaint that Obama is an anti-American Socialist is slightly off. Obama has a twisted affection for his country, even as he harms America at every turn, and Socialism isn't really the point for him, even though most of his policies are Socialist. For D'Souza, the anti-colonial theory explains everything that Obama does as president, including the moments when he pretends to be a healer to keep the façade going. Obama is "dedicated to a campaign of revenge" on behalf of his defeated father: "Obama is on a systematic campaign against the colonial system that destroyed his father's dreams. With a kind of suppressed fury, he is committed to keep going until he has brought that system down. And according to his father's anti-colonial ideology, which Obama has internalized for himself, that system is the military and economic power of the United States of America."[17]

In D'Souza's telling, *Dreams from My Father* is a revelation of Obama's commitment to destroy everything smacking of Western colonialism. Thus, Obama gave it an unusual title, stressing "from." Obama's mother, D'Souza says, taught Obama to idolize his father, and she had anti-American prejudices to match. As a youth, Obama imbibed the anti-colonial folklore of Hawaii and Indonesia. The defining moment of Obama's youth was the day that his father explained anti-colonialism to Obama's 5th-grade class. As a student, Obama consumed a diet of "oppression studies," D'Souza's moniker for American liberal arts education. Upon making his pilgrimage to Kenya, Obama dedicated himself to fulfilling his father's dream, which filled him with hatred, "but it was a calm hatred, an ideological hatred" of the system and social hierarchies that Western colonialism created. This hateful dream consumes Obama and his presidency, D'Souza contends: "It is a dream that, as president, he is imposing with a vengeance on America and the world."[18]

As a domestic policy, D'Souza explains, post-colonialism is always about humbling the overclass by subordinating it to the power of government. Obama is obsessed with sticking it to the rich, although, admittedly, Obama is not as stridently anti-capitalist as his father was. D'Souza notes that Obama's father was a post-colonial African Socialist—not a Communist—who wanted to use the power of the state to take over the economy and to abolish everything that remained of British rule in Kenya. The elder Obama clashed with Jomo Kenyatta over Socialism versus capitalism, demanding a Kenyan state that nationalized the means of production. In D'Souza's telling, Obama, like his father, wants to use the power of the state to bring down the overclass. But for Obama, Socialist ideology is not indispensable for this purpose. Obama is comfortable with corporate capitalists, he persuaded the insurance companies to support health reform, and he provided millions of new customers to them. D'Souza reasons that Obama is happy to deal with the capitalist class as long as it is willing "to succumb to a government leash and to being told what to do by Big Daddy Obama."[19]

In foreign affairs, in this telling, Obama-style anti-colonialism is equally straightforward, though operating in reverse, seeking to diminish American power. D'Souza claims that Obama does not want to win the war in Afghanistan; in fact, Obama wants the United States to lose in Afghanistan, to strike a blow for anti-colonialism: "His only concern is how fast he can get America out." The only reason that Obama escalated in Afghanistan was to provide political cover for his anti-imperial animus to get the United States out of the Muslim world. Similarly, D'Souza contends, Obama does not care if Iran and North Korea attain nuclear weapons; his only concern in this area is to lesson the nuclear capability of the United States and its allies.[20]

That would seem to convict Obama of anti-Americanism too, but D'Souza wants to be fair. Obama has an affection of some kind for the country that lifted him to power, D'Souza allows. To be sure, Obama does hate Republicans—"They are not just wrong; they are evil." Obama's nice talk about civility and working together are just for show; Obama regards Republicans as the enemy, the neo-colonial party. Working with them would be pointless. But D'Souza acknowledges that Obama does not hate his country. At least, Obama does not hate his fantasy of what America should become—a humbled, mediocre, post-colonial nation that does not think of itself as an exception to history. D'Souza explains that Obama regards himself as a defender of America's interests, because he thinks that America and the world would be better off if the United States lost its great power. This vision of the United States is apparently therapeutic for Obama's twisted psyche, D'Souza observes, "but it is a ridiculous one for America in the twenty-first century."[21]

The anti-colonial thesis ostensibly explains Obama's determination to expand government power at home and to diminish American power abroad. According to D'Souza, it also explains why Obama seems "so distant, detached, and even bored." It is draining enough to have to act white for the public, but Obama has an extremely eccentric and advanced case of the "acting white" problem. Obama is caught in a time machine, D'Souza contends. He has no real connection to American history. Even his relationship to the Civil Rights movement is totally contrived for a political purpose, not something that he feels. At the level of feeling and imagination, Obama reads himself into a different story, the Mau Mau rebellion in Kenya, which the British crushed with vicious brutality. For Obama, D'Souza argues, the story that matters is the battle of African guerilla movements against Europe's marauding colonial armies. Obama yearns for the heroic grandeur and moral clarity of the black Africans who stood up against their white oppressors. George Washington pales by comparison, as does the "dull and thin" world of global summits to which Obama drags himself as President of the United States.[22]

Take a breath. Obama's life and presidency are consumed with rage and revenge? He does not think like an American or identify with the United States? He is bored by the presidency? The Civil Rights movement means nothing to him? He does not believe in American liberal democracy? He escalated in Afghanistan and Pakistan in order to strangle American power? He laments, daydreaming in the West Wing, that he didn't get to fight the British in Kenya in 1952? What is beyond ludicrous?

D'Souza says that Obama is crafty in spreading his anti-colonial poison, such as, after the Gulf of Mexico oil spill: "Time and again he condemned 'British Petroleum'—an interesting term since the company long ago changed its name to BP." Fascinating, except that Obama never said "British Petroleum" in the event that D'Souza describes, let alone time and again. Straining to tag Obama, of all people, as an advocate of racial revenge, D'Souza descends to a level of race-baiting that would have embarrassed Lee Atwater or George Wallace. He misrepresents *Dreams from My Father* to the point of standing the book on its head. Somehow, in D'Souza's telling, Obama absorbed anti-colonial vengeance from a father that he idolized, never mind that Obama met his father only once; he knew very little about him throughout his youth; in his memoir, he described the pain that he felt upon learning about his father's life; and D'Souza has no theory about how Obama internalized his father's ostensible ideology.[23]

Above all, it is perverse to stigmatize Obama as an obsessed anti-colonialist on the evidence that his writings contain critical remarks about imperialism. The United States was founded as an anti-colonial rebellion, and Obama says nothing about empire or colonialism that is not standard fare for liberal Democrats. Obama's most radical position is something that he shares with Harry Truman and Richard Nixon—that the poor and vulnerable should be provided with health coverage. Since Obama has the same ideology as John Kerry and Hillary Clinton, what is the point of making him out as a vengeful anti-colonialist who wants to put whitey down and take whitey's money?

But that question answers itself, and Gingrich embraced the answer as a platform for a presidential candidacy. D'Souza's account was, to Gingrich, profound, brilliant, and utterly convincing. Gingrich told *National Review Online* that to understand Obama, one has to understand "Kenyan, anti-colonial behavior"; otherwise, Obama is "outside our comprehension," exactly as he likes it: "This is a person who is fundamentally out of touch with how the world works, who happened to have played a wonderful con, as a result of which he is now president." Gingrich charged that Obama is "authentically dishonest," a trick that he mastered as an Alinsky-style community organizer: "He was being the person he needed to be in order to achieve the position he needed to achieve." For absurdity, it would be hard to top this particular politician presuming moral superiority over this president.²⁴

Things are not so bad that Donald Trump or Newt Gingrich can ride naked race-baiting to the presidency. Mitt Romney and most of the Republican contenders try to steer clear of it as they compete for the Republican nomination. But they are competing for the favor of a Republican base that wants to believe ludicrous things about Obama.

The good society

In 1985, a few years into the Reagan era, a group of academics led by sociologist Robert Bellah tried to account for what was happening to America morally, socially, and politically. Bellah's co-authors were Richard Madsen, William M. Sullivan, Ann Swidler, and Steven M. Tipton; the book they wrote was *Habits of the Heart: Individualism and Commitment in American Life*. In the wake of Reagan's massive electoral victory over Walter Mondale, a symbol of New Deal liberalism, the Bellah group disputed Reagan's campaign slogan that it was "morning in America."²⁵

The Bellah group countered that America was wracked with terrible problems of economic injustice and moral cynicism. In the past, they argued, the anti-social ravages of American individualism were mitigated by the influence of Biblical religion and civic republicanism in American life. These moral languages taught an ethic of community stewardship and provided a litmus test for assessing a society's moral health. The test was how society deals with the cluster of problems pertaining to wealth and poverty. Scripture condemns inequality and oppression, taking the side of the poor against the principalities and powers that exploit them. Republican theory from Aristotle to the American founders assumed that a free society could survive only if there is an approximate equality of opportunity and condition among citizens.

The Bellah group acknowledged that these moral convictions had always been contested in the United States. But now they were being erased from America's cultural memory. American youth no longer knew or cared about the biblical sources of the American experiment or the social gospel dream of a cooperative commonwealth. A new and largely unchurched American generation voted for Reagan and cheered his broadsides against liberalism, the welfare state, the feminist and peace movements, the mainline churches, and the unions. The dominant trend in American life, according to the Bellah group, was toward an atomized society that reduced all moral and social issues to the languages of possessive or expressive individualism. In national politics, the triumph of Reaganism symbolized this trend, just as Reagan himself mythologized it.

Habits of the Heart struck a cultural nerve. The book's portrait of an increasingly rootless and narcissistic American middle class was heralded as a telling critique of the loss of community in American life. In the academy, the book fueled an upsurge of communitarian social theory, which began with Michael Sandel's landmark critique of the liberal ideology of the "unencumbered self," *Liberalism and the Limits of Justice* (1982). Communitarians criticized the egocentrism of America's dominant culture, contending that American conservatism and liberalism were overly preoccupied with individual rights and individual success. Both of America's dominant political traditions eroded the connections between individuals and their families, communities, and nations. Both traditions rationalized the assaults of global capitalism on communities, mediating institutions, and the environment. Communitarians resurrected John Dewey's understanding of democracy as a "great community" of shared values and his conception of politics as the project of continually re-creating the public. The more progressive versions of communitarian theory followed the Bellah group in stressing the wealth and poverty test of a society's moral health.[26]

To be sure, *Habits of the Heart* had many flaws and limitations. It was decidedly focused on the moral condition of professionally oriented, middle-class, mostly white Americans. The book lauded Martin Luther King, Jr. as an exemplar of the U.S. best moral traditions, but it offered no account of the African-American culture that produced him. It took a liberal feminist perspective for granted without discussing feminism or the implications of its argument for feminism. It could be read as a nostalgic lament for a lost Christian America, even as the Bellah group disavowed that reading. The book seemed strangely removed from important debates of the time over racial, cultural, and sexual politics. These drawbacks made the book ripe for hijacking by conservatives who waved off its animating concern with social justice.[27]

With all its limitations in method and perspective, however, *Habits of the Heart* portrayed the eclipse of moral community in the United States in ways that reflected far beyond its focus on upwardly mobile white professionals. The Bellah group stressed that many Americans no longer took ethical instruction from character shaping communities of any kind. Asked to explain their moral values, Americans increasingly fell back on their society's ethos of the sovereign consumer. The religious and republican moral languages of America's past were being displaced by an individualistic pursuit of success or emotional satisfaction that placed highly tenuous selves at the center of a meaningless world.

Moreover, the Bellah group cautioned that this sorry picture affected not only those who belonged to no community. Even for most Americans who identified with some religious, cultural, or political community, the ethic of individual rights and success provided the primary operative frame of moral reference. For the Christian Right, American capitalism folded seamlessly into the Christian gospel. Mainline churches, on the other hand, struggling to stay in business, took the therapeutic option, providing undemanding communities of care for religious consumers and preaching an innocuous gospel that threatened nobody.

Habits of the Heart called for a renewal of morally generative communities of memory that cared about social justice. It warned that the erosion of America's religious and democratic traditions had seriously weakened the force of the biblical/republican ethic in American life. Many Americans claimed to believe that poverty could be alleviated by private charity. This belief was closely tied to the dominant American dream of becoming a star, a dream assiduously promoted by commercial culture. The Bellah group contrasted two American dreams, both deeply rooted in U.S. American history. In the dominant dream, one attained enough success to stand apart from others, not have to worry about them, and perhaps look down on them. The second dream was that of living in a good society, "a society that would really be worth living in."[28]

A good society would subordinate private interest to the common good, the Bellah group argued. It would reduce the punishments of failure and the rewards of success. It would resist the relentless capitalist drive to turn labor and nature into commodities. It would expand opportunities for socially useful work and promote economic democracy by expanding the cooperative and community-development sectors. It would recognize that commercial society is at war with the world's natural ecology and its social ecology. *Habits of the Heart* called for a new social ecology that strengthened the social ties that bind human beings to each other.

That came right to the edge of saying, twenty-six years ago, what must be said today—that American democracy and the world's ecology are being routed by the unsustainable demands of corporate capitalism. The Earth's ecosystem cannot sustain a U.S. American-level lifestyle for more than one-fifth of the world's population. The economy is physical. There are limits to economic growth. Global warming is melting the Arctic ice cap at a shocking pace, as well as large areas of permafrost in Alaska, Canada, and Siberia, and destroying wetlands and forests around the world. Everything on the planet that is frozen is melting. We have to find alternatives to a system that constantly demands more freedom for itself to pile up more wealth for the few while treating the destructive aspects of its activity as somebody else's problem.

The Bellah group did not foresee twenty years of unleashed greed in the financial sector. It did not foresee the abolition of the Glass-Steagall wall separating commercial banks and investment firms, or Wall Street's soaring traffic in derivatives. Yet it saw the problem clearly enough to write a sequel, *The Good Society* (1991), that stressed the necessity of creating structural alternatives to corporate capitalism. *The Good Society* made a programmatic argument for expanding the cooperative sector, reducing the anxiety and cynicism of economic life, building a movement for economic democracy, and helping people to be secure enough to make commitments to each other and pursue activities that are good in themselves.[29]

Shrewdly, the Bellah group insisted that its social vision passed Reinhold Niebuhr's tests for realism. They appealed to Niebuhr's passion for justice, his commitment to democracy, his emphasis on the limits of politics, and his commitment to re-creating the public. They portrayed Niebuhr's work as an important corrective to Dewey's idealistic liberalism, suggesting that Niebuhr was right about the inevitability of violence and collective egotism. The Bellah group accepted Niebuhr's thesis that politics is about the struggle of competing interests for self-promoting power. Movements based on ethical concern for the common good or religiously inspired good will do not change structures of power. In the social arena, power can only be challenged by power.

The Bellah group absorbed these lessons deeply enough to understand that they could not simply return to a pre-Niebuhrian progressivism. The social gospel movement mistakenly thought that a cooperative commonwealth was literally achievable, partly because it refused to accept that group egotism is inevitable. Any worthwhile social ethic had to absorb Niebuhr's point that every social gain creates the possibility of new forms of social evil.

To the Bellah group, however, relinquishing the idea of a good society on these grounds was a non-starter, no matter what Niebuhr said against it. The common good emerges from discussion and struggle. It is never settled definitively. But some idea of it is necessary to provide a vision of what is worth struggling for and to test the boundaries of possibility. The Bellah group observed that in the dominant version of the American dream, there is no such thing as a good society or the common good. There is only the sum of individual goods. The sum of individual goods, however, when organized only by capitalism, eventually produces a common bad that destroys personal goods along with society.

We have accumulated a staggering common bad since the Bellah group wrote its books on the common good. Celebrants of neo-liberal globalization exaggerated the futility of political attempts to channel economic forces. They were far too credulous about the self-correcting capacities of the market, which supposedly made it unnecessary to regulate banks and investment firms. They waved off the huge imbalances between economies relying on debt-financed consumption and those promoting over-saving and production-oriented exports. Above all, they wrongly supposed that America's widening chasm between productivity and wages could be bridged with more and more borrowing. In 1955, corporate taxes yielded 27 percent of federal revenue; by the end of the Bush Administration, that figure was down to 9 percent, and giant corporations like Boeing, General Electric, Verizon, and Citigroup paid no taxes at all—erasing even the memory that it wasn't always so.

Community and meaning
The progressive communitarian perspective I have just explicated is, to be sure, well to the left of Obama's. Some forms of communitarian

theory place a high value on authority, and some are politically moderate forms of "third way" politics in which communitarianism becomes a vague rationale for "responsibility," usually defined as the political middle ground, wherever it happens to be. Obama is skilled at bending communitarian thought to the latter purpose, aiming at the middle ground where every national election is decided. But Obama is a communitarian, mostly of a progressive-leaning type. His thought was shaped in the 1980s and early 1990s when debates over communitarian criticism re-energized the field of political theory.

Obama is devoted to a deliberative politics of the common good that builds up new and old communities of memory to achieve a good society. The civic republican language of identity, pragmatic engagement, civil society, and communities of faith is second nature to him. It was the basis of his work as a community organizer, which led him to join a Christian community. It is the basis of everything that he says about the optimum relationship between politics and religion. It is the basis of his insistence that freedom, equality, and community go together in a healthy society. It is the basis of his untiring insistence that common solutions have to be found that mediate rival ideological positions. Harvard intellectual historian James Kloppenberg aptly observes, "Obama understands that the power of our principles of liberty and equality depends not on the fervor with which they are proclaimed but on the deliberative process from which they are developed. That process requires us to debate, test, and revise the meaning of our ideals in practice rather then genuflecting reverentially before them."[30]

Democracy is the work of practically and continually renewing society. Obama had an astute and reflective grasp of it as an organizer, as he showed in an article for *Illinois Issues* in 1988. This article, "Why Organize? Problems and Promise in the Inner City," had some clunky sentences lacking noun-verb agreement that later evoked sneers from anti-Obama bloggers. But those who claim that Obama was incapable of writing his two books overlook that he never had a speechwriter before he became famous, he wrote every sentence of the 2004 convention barnburner that launched his fame, and his early article on organizing bore the marks of his later thought and style. For Obama, communitarian theory helped to make sense of long-running debates among African-Americans over integration versus nationalism, accommodation versus militancy, and Booker T. Washington versus W. E. B. DuBois. By the 1980s, Obama observed, these historic debates usually played out as an argument between advocates of economic self-development and electoral politics. In Chicago, the black community was pretty much stalemated over this binary choice until Harold Washington swept to the mayor's office in 1983, after which the party politics group had four years of glory and pride. Then, Washington died, and the old stalemate returned.[31]

Obama held out for the community-organizing alternative to a bad choice between self-help and going political. There had to be a way to hold together the strengths of the two predominant approaches, he urged. The community-organizing strategy proposed that there are solutions to the grinding problems of inner-city communities, that these communities only lack the power that is necessary to solve their problems, and that the only way to build up power that makes a difference is to organize people and money around a common vision. Doing it requires building up broad-based organizations that unite religious congregations, block groups, parent associations, and similar groups. Obama implored that every obstacle to building such organizations is a reason why they are needed. To build one is to gain voice and power for the needs of communities, breaking the "crippling isolation" that makes poor and vulnerable people believe that there is no solution. Community organizing, Obama concluded with a rhetorical flourish, brings out the beauty and strength of ordinary human beings: "Through the songs of the church and the talk on the stoops, through the hundreds of individual stories of coming up from the South and finding any job that would pay, of raising families on threadbare budgets, of losing some children to drugs and watching others earn degrees and land jobs their parents could never aspire to—it is through these stories and songs of dashed hopes and powers of endurance, of ugliness and strife, subtlety and laughter, that organizers can shape a sense of community not only for others, but for themselves."[32]

Eighteen years later, now as a U.S. Senator, Obama addressed a conference on "Building a Covenant for a New America," sponsored by Jim Wallis' "Call to Renewal" organization and *Sojourners* magazine. Most of his keynote speech was straight out of *The Audacity of Hope,* which was about to be published. In both places, he expounded on the difference between being religiously faithful in an open-ended way and claiming religious certainty in a publicly problematic way. Obama stressed that he was "anchored" in his faith, but not rigid or dogmatic about it. Here as elsewhere, he walked a tightrope between saying more than one should say as a public official and not saying anything to avoid controversy. Too many Democrats took the path of saying as little as possible, even when they had a religious faith to cover up. Obama admitted that he took that tack in his 2004 Senate race, which nagged at him. Faced with a far-out opponent who made dramatic statements about how Jesus Christ would vote, Obama stayed off the religious issue and waited for election day.[33]

But that ceded the religious issue to conservatives like Alan Keyes and Pat Robertson. Obama realized that he needed to do better than that. At the conference, though not in the book, he put it directly—in a passage that echoed *Habits of the Heart* and Harvard sociologist Robert Putnam's research on the dwindling social capital of Americans. Putnam reported that Americans were increasingly isolated, lacking vital ties to social or community networks of any kind; in his arresting image, "bowling alone" had become commonplace. Obama replied that human beings need meaning and connection even when they behave otherwise. Something terribly important is missing in the busyness and materialism of modern American life, he argued. Busy materialism violates the spiritual nature of human beings. Obama contended that most people want a sense of purpose, "a narrative arc to their lives," even if they keep to themselves, numb themselves to the world, and bowl alone: "They're looking to relieve a chronic loneliness, a feeling supported by a recent study that shows Americans have fewer close friends and confidants than ever before. And so they need an assurance that somebody out there cares about them, is listening to them—that they are not just destined to travel down a long highway towards nothingness."[34]

He acknowledged that he spoke from experience. He grew up with no religious faith or community, and when he worked as an organizer with Christians in Chicago, he sang their songs and shared their values: "But they sensed a part of me that remained removed, detached, an observer in their midst. In time, I too came to realize that something was missing—that without a vessel for my beliefs, without a commitment to a particular community of faith, at some level I would always remain apart and alone."[35]

By then, heading into a presidential campaign, Obama had become adept at talking about his spiritual sensibility. On the campaign trail, he readily found his preacher voice. Later, running the country, it was harder to find or, at least, it was harder to find occasions to use it. There were notable exceptions. Obama's audience at the Nobel Prize speech was intently quiet through most of the speech, but near the end, he jolted the secular Norwegians into an emotional standing ovation with his peroration about reaching for the world that ought to be, "that spark of the divine that still stirs within each of our souls." On January 12, 2011, speaking to a grieving and polarized community and nation, Obama the pastor re-emerged.

Four days earlier, Arizona Rep. Gabrielle Giffords had convened one of her regular outdoor gatherings, which she called "Congress on Your Corner," outside a supermarket in Tuscan. A gunman, Jared Lee Loughner, drew a pistol, shot Giffords in the head, and opened fire on the crowd of approximately 25 people. Six people were killed and thirteen were wounded; Giffords was critically wounded. A bitter national controversy erupted over gun control and the toxic political atmosphere surrounding immigration and health reform. Loughner had used a 9-mm Glock-19 semi-automatic pistol with a 33-round magazine that he purchased legally, despite years of emotional turmoil, and Giffords had received threats for taking liberal positions on immigration and health reform. A few months earlier, Giffords had noted on MSNBC that Sarah Palin's published target list for the 2010 election depicted the crosshairs of a gunsight over Giffords' district. Giffords protested, "When people do that, they have got to realize there are consequences to that action." In the aftermath of the shooting, Pima County Sheriff Clarence Dupnik declared at a press conference: "When you look at unbalanced people, how they respond to the vitriol that comes out of certain mouths about tearing down the government—the anger, the hatred, the bigotry that goes on in this country is getting to be outrageous. And unfortunately, Arizona, I think, has become the capital. We have become the mecca for prejudice and bigotry."[36]

Loughner's ability to buy a semi-automatic and fire over twenty shots in a few seconds was one issue. The prevailing atmosphere of hatefulness and bigotry was another. Dupnik's suggestion that this massacre had some connection to Tea Party activism was something else, and not helpful or true. Obama walked into a cauldron of grief and anger in Tucson, acknowledging immediately that nothing he could say would "fill the sudden hole torn in your hearts." He applied Psalm 46 to Tucson: "God is within her, she will not fail." He moved, in a pastoral fashion, through the roll of the slain, making personal remarks about each victim, ending with a nine-year-old girl, Christina Taylor Green. He reported that Giffords had opened her eyes that day; in the manner of black church repetition, he said it four times.[37]

And he spoke against the accusatory mode. "Scripture tells us that there is evil in the world, and that terrible things happen for reasons that defy human understanding." It was imperative not to rush to simple explanations and accusations, he implored: "For the truth is none of us can know exactly what triggered this vicious attack. None of us can know with any certainty what might have stopped these shots from being fired, or what thoughts lurked in the inner recesses of a violent man's mind. Yes, we have to examine all the facts behind this tragedy. We cannot and will not be passive in the face of such violence. We should be willing to challenge old assumptions in order to lessen the prospects of such violence in the future. But what we cannot do is use this tragedy as one more occasion to turn on each other. That we cannot do. That we cannot do."

When we suffer tragedies, Obama observed, we are awakened to our mortality. We remember that we have only a little while on this Earth and that in this fleeting time, "what matters is not wealth, or status, or power, or fame—but rather, how well we have loved and what small part we have played in making the lives of other people better." He had a black church "close," a take-home message about Christina jumping in rain puddles in heaven, but before Obama got there, he had a quintessentially Obama pre-close: "We may not be able to stop all evil in the world, but I know that how we treat one another, that's entirely up to us. And I believe that for all our imperfections, we are full of decency and goodness, and that the forces that divide us are not as strong as those that unite us."

What kind of country?

What kind of country should the United States want to be? For two centuries, Americans have given two fundamentally different answers to this question. The first is the vision of a society that provides unrestricted liberty to acquire wealth. The second is the vision of a realized democracy in which democratic rights over society's major institutions are established. In the first vision, the right to property is lifted above the right to self-government, and the just society minimizes the equalizing role of government. In the second view, the right to self-government is considered superior to the right to property, and the just society places democratic checks on social, political, and economic power.[38]

Both of these visions are ideal types, deeply rooted in U.S. American history, that reflect inherent tensions between classic liberalism and democracy. Both have limited and conditioned each other in the U.S. American experience. But in every generation, one of them gains predominance over the other, shaping the terms of political possibility. From 1980 to 2008, the unleashed capitalist vision prevailed in American politics. Now, we are in a national conversation about whether capitalism or democracy should have the upper hand.

To the founders that wrote the U.S. constitution, "liberal" was a good word, referring to the liberties of white male property owners, while "democracy" was a scare word, referring to the vengeance and stupidity of the mob. From the beginning, democratic movements countered that liberty must be fused with democracy. The building blocks of American liberal democracy emerged from the early struggles between the parties of liberty and democracy: an open society, checks and balances, enumerated powers, consent of the governed, due process, the republican safeguards of *Federalist* Number Ten, separation of church and state, and disagreements over who deserved to be enfranchised, whether liberty could tolerate much democracy, and whether the American idea included republican democracy or a strong federal state.

In the nineteenth century, the Jeffersonian/Jacksonian party of democracy prevailed about republican democracy; the Federalist/Whig party of the state prevailed about a federal state; both parties compounded the U.S. original sins against Native Americans and African-Americans; the Republican Party emerged to challenge chattel slavery; and the Progressive movement embraced the idea of a centralized government. The latter development turned the party of democracy into the party of the state, changing the meaning of "liberal" in American politics. Before the Progressive era, the Federalist/Whig/Republican tradition stood for the consolidation of the national union, while Jacksonian and populist democrats stood for decentralized power, small-town values, and farming interests. The Progressive movement changed this picture by democratizing liberal ideology. Progressives converted to national governance, laying the groundwork for the New Deal, while Republicans became the party of anti-government individualism and big business.[39]

The party of democracy, despite its racist and sexist history, made gains for social justice by demanding that society recognizes the rights and humanity of groups lacking privileged status. The logic of democracy put the question to privileged groups: Why should only you have access to education, property, wealth, health care, and other social goods?

Democracy and the common good go together. Obama did not exaggerate when he spoke at Tom Harkin's steak fry in 2006: The unleashed capitalist vision of the Republican Party is about dismantling democratic governance. It is about breaking up government piece by piece, privatizing Social Security and Medicare, abolishing programs for the poor and vulnerable, cutting taxes for corporations and the wealthy, abolishing public schools, replacing police with private security guards, letting Wall Street do whatever it wants, and turning public parks into privately owned playgrounds. Obama rightly stressed that this vision of a society favoring the interests of corporations and the rich lies behind almost everything that Republicans do in Congress. It is the view that America is at its best when Americans deny that they owe obligations to each other.

Obama stopped putting it this starkly after he won the presidency, because he had no chance of winning Republican cooperation on anything if he did not tell Republicans that he expected better than that. In his 2010 State of the Union Address, he told Republican leaders that if they were going to insist that no business could get done in the Senate without sixty votes, they had to take responsibility for governing: "Just saying no to everything may be good short-term politics, but it's not leadership. We were sent here to serve our citizens, not our ambitions. So let's show the American people that we can do it together."[40]

He knows that cooperation across party lines to solve the nation's problems will not happen, yet he keeps calling for it. Obama wants to be the Ronald Reagan of his party, a forward-looking optimist who changes the course of history. He wants to do it by winning independents and a significant minority of Republicans to his idea of good government, just as Reagan won over independents and the Blue Dog Democrats. But nobody doubted where Reagan stood ideologically, and Obama has no chance of winning anything more than token Republican cooperation. Reagan was the most ideologically defined president of the past half-century and the only ideological movement leader to be elected president. Obama doubts that his worldview serves him as well. To succeed, he believes, he must keep proving that he cares more about civility and cooperation than about fighting for a principle.

He may, indeed, win a second term by sticking to this script. But the big issues that loom ahead will have to be fought over, because America cannot build a clean energy economy, rebuild the nation's infrastructure, make massive investments in education, lift the cap on Social Security, break the financial oligarchy, and scale back the military empire on Republican terms. The big things that must be done contradict Republican ideology. Even defending the financial and healthcare reforms that Obama has achieved will require more fighting than he put up to attain them. Obama wants to "win the future" by inspiring Americans to believe that they can still do big things. Surely, he implores, America can build new airports like the Chinese and build fast trains like the Europeans and Chinese.[41]

But to win the future, the party of the common good must struggle with conviction for a just society, telling a galvanizing story about the struggle for it. The saddest irony of Obama's presidency is that he has fallen short on conveying what he believes in and is willing to fight for. Campaigning in 2008, Obama was eloquent and inspiring, using his story to paint a vision of America's vibrant, cosmopolitan, communitarian future. Governing afterward, he mostly coped and adapted, leaving his supporters perplexed about where he wanted to take the nation. Obama is still the most compelling human being to reach the White House in decades and a figure of singular promise for the progressive transformation of American politics and society. But to fulfill that promise, he has to overcome his own cautious, accommodating temperament, helping to mobilize a movement for social justice and the common good.

Today, America's super-wealthy either pay no income taxes at all or pay very little while treating themselves mostly to the capital gains rate—all perfectly legally, owing to the favors that Washington showers on the super-wealthy. Investment managers earning billions of dollars per year are allowed to classify their income as carried interest, which is taxed at the same rate as capital gains. Constantly, we are told that the investor class would lose its zeal for making money if it had to pay taxes on its actual income or if the capital gain rates were raised. But this assurance does not pass the laugh test, and there is no evidence for it. Investment tycoon Warren Buffett, after 60 years of working with investors, reports that he has never met one who shied away from making a promising investment because of the tax rate on a potential gain.[42]

A tax system that serves the common good would have additional brackets for the highest incomes, as the United States once did. It would have a bracket for $1 million earners and a bracket for $10 million dollar earners and a bracket for $100 million earners and so on. It would lift the cap on the Social Security tax, taxing salaries above $102,000 per year, or at least, as Obama proposed in 2008, creating a "doughnut hole" that adds a Social Security tax for individuals earning more than $250,000. And it would facilitate creative planning for economic democracy.

If we can spend trillions of taxpayer dollars bailing out banks and setting up "bad bank" contraptions to eat their toxic debt, we ought to be able to create good public banks at the state and federal levels to do good things. A national infrastructure bank, once created, would get serious money plowed into infrastructure rebuilding on an ongoing basis. Public banks could finance start-ups in green technology that are currently languishing and provide financing for cooperatives that traditional banks spurn. They can be established at the state level, following the leads of North Dakota and Washington, to create state credit machines not dependent on Wall Street. They can be established at the federal level by Congressional mandate or by claiming the good assets of banks seized by the government, or both.

These would be very good projects for a second term, spurring a realignment that is long overdue.

Notes

1. See V. O Key, "A Theory of Critical Elections," *Journal of Politics* 17 (1955), pp. 3–18; Walter Dean Burnham, 1970, *Critical Elections and the Mainsprings of American Politics*, New York:

Norton; Burnham, "Periodization Schemes and 'Party Systems': The 'System of 1896' as a Case in Point," *Social Science History* 10 (August 1986), 263–314; Paul Kleppner (Westport, CT: Greenwood, 1981); Jerome M. Clubb, William H. Flanigan, and Nancy H. Zingale, 1980, *Partisan Realignment: Voters, Parties, and Government in American History*, Beverly Hills, CA: Sage Publications. Parts of this chapter adapt material from Gary Dorrien, "The Common Good," *Christian Century* (April 19, 2011), and Dorrien, *Economy, Difference, Empire: Social Ethics for Social Justice* (New York: Columbia University Press, 2010), pp. 145–152.

2. See Edward N. Wolff, 1996, *Top Heavy*, New York: New Press; Wolf, "Recent Trends in Household Wealth in the United States: Rising Debt and the Middle-Class Squeeze—An Update to 2007," *Working Paper No. 589* (Annandale-on-Hudson, NY: Levy Economics Institute of Bard College, 2010); Kevin Phillips, 1990, *The Politics of Rich and Poor*, New York: Random House; Joseph E. Stiglitz, "Of the 1%, by the 1%, for the 1%," *Vanity Fair* (May 2011); G. William Domhoff, 1990, *The Power Elite and the State: How Policy is Made in America* (Hawthorne, NY: Aldine de Gruyter).

3. See Eamonn Fingleton, 2003, *Unsustainable: How Economic Dogma Is Destroying American Prosperity*, New York: Nation Books; Doug Henwood, *After the New Economy* (New York: New Press, 2005); Barry Bluestone and Bennett Harrison, 1982, *The Deindustrialization of America: Plant Closings, Community Abandonment, and the Dismantling of Basic Industry*, New York: Basic Books; Michael J. Piore and Charles E. Sabel, 1984, *The Second Industrial Divide: Possibilities for Prosperity*, New York: Basic Books.

4. Thomas L. Friedman, 2000, *The Lexus and the Olive Tree: Understanding Globalization*, New York: Anchor Books; Friedman, 2005, *The World Is Flat: A Brief History of the Twenty-First Century*, New York: Farrar, Straus and Giroux; Jagdish Bhagwati, 2004, *In Defense of Globalization*, New York: Oxford University Press.

5. Congressional Budget Office, "CBO Report: Estimated Impact of the American Recovery and Reinvestment Act on Employment and Economic Output from April 2010 through June 2010," (August 2010), Washington, DC.

6. Brad O'Leary, 2008, *The Audacity of Deceit: Barack Obama's War on American Values*, Los Angeles: WND Books; Aaron Klein, *The Manchurian President: Barack Obama's Ties to Communists, Socialists, and Other Anti-American Extremists* (Washington, DC: WND Books, 2010); Michelle Malkin, 2009, *Culture of Corruption: Obama and His Team of Tax Cheats, Crooks, and Cronies*, Washington, DC: Regnery; Pamela Geller (with Robert Spencer) *The Post-American Presidency: The Obama Administration's War on America* (New York: Threshold Editions, 2010); Webster Griffon Tarpley, *Obama: The Postmodern Coup* (Joshua Tree, CA: Progressive Press, 2008); Jack Cashill, 2011, *Deconstructing Obama*, New York: Threshold Editions, Simon & Schuster; see Max Blumenthal, "Queen of the Birthers," *The Daily Beast* (July 30, 2009), http://www.thedailybeast.com; Cashill, "Is Khalid al-Mansour the Man Behind Obama Myth?" *WorldNetDaily* (August 28, 2008), http://www.wnd.com.

7. Jerome R. Corsi, 2008, *The Obama Nation: Leftist Politics and the Cult of Personality*, New York: Threshold Editions; John E. O'Neill and Jerome R. Corsi, 2004, *Unfit for Command: Swift Boat Veterans Speak Out Against John Kerry*, Washington, DC: Regnery; "MMFA Investigates: Who is Jerome Corsi, co-author of Swift Boat Vets Attack Book?" Media Matters (August 6, 2008), http://mediamatters.org/research/200408060010; quotes; Kenneth P. Vogel, "Wild Theories of 'Obama Nation' Author," *Politico* (August 13, 2008), http://www.politico.com.

8. Jerome R. Corsi, 2007, *The Late Great USA: The Coming Merger with Mexico and Canada*, Los Angeles: WND Books; Corsi, *The Obama Nation: Leftist Politics and the Cult of Personality*, quote x.
9. Barack Obama, "I'm Here Because Somebody Marched," Brown Chapel A.M.E. Church, Selma, Alabama (March 4, 2007), http://www.youtube.com.
10. Corsi, *The Obama Nation: Leftist Politics and the Cult of Personality*, quote 33.
11. Barack Obama, *Dreams from My Father: A Story of Race and Inheritance* (1995; New York: Three Rivers Press, 2004), 51; Corsi, *The Obama Nation: Leftist Politics and the Cult of Personality*, 65-6, 82-3; Richard Cohen, "Obama's Back Story," *Washington Post* (March 27, 2007); Kristen Scharnberg and Kim Barker, "The not-so-simple story of Barack Obama's youth," *Chicago Tribune* (March 25, 2007); Frantz Fanon, 1967, *Black Skin, White Masks*, New York: Grove.
12. Corsi, *The Obama Nation: Leftist Politics and the Cult of Personality*, 70–91.
13. Ibid., quotes 230, 233; Jerome R. Corsi, *Where's the Birth Certificate?: The Case that Barack Obama Is Not Eligible to Be President* (Washington, DC: WND Books, 2011).
14. Corsi, *The Obama Nation: Leftist Politics and the Cult of Personality*, 80–84.
15. Dinesh D'Souza, "How Obama Thinks," *Forbes* (September 27, 2010).
16. Dinesh D'Souza, *The Roots of Obama's Rage* (Washington, DC: Regnery Publishing, 2010), quote 19.
17. Ibid., quote 199.
18. Ibid., quotes 127, 35.
19. Ibid., quote 172.
20. Ibid., quotes 52, 55.
21. Ibid., quotes 170, 218.
22. Ibid., quotes 198, 199.
23. Ibid., quote 47.
24. Robert Costa, "Gingrich: Obama's 'Kenyan, anti-colonial Worldview," *National Review Online* (September 11, 2010), http://www.nationalreview.com.
25. Robert Bellah, Richard Madsen, William M. Sullivan, Ann Swidler, and Steven M. Tipton, *Habits of the Heart: Individualism and Commitment in American Life* (Berkeley: University of California Press, 1985; third edition, 2008).
26. Michael Sandel, 1982, *Liberalism and the Limits of Justice*, Cambridge: Cambridge University Press; see William Sullivan, 1982, *Reconstructing Public Philosophy*, Berkeley: University of California Press; Michael Walzer, 1985, *Spheres of Justice A Defense of Pluralism and Equality*, New York: Basic Books; Alasdair MacIntyre, 1984, *After Virtue: A Study in Moral Theory*, Notre Dame: University of Notre Dame; Amitai Etzioni, 1993, *The Spirit of Community: Rights, Responsibilities, and the Communitarian Agenda*, New York: Crown Publishers.
27. See Vincent Harding, "Toward a Darkly Radiant Vision of America's Truth: A Letter of Concern, An Invitation to Re-Creation," in *Community in America: The Challenge of Habits of the Heart* (Berkeley: University of California Press, 1988), pp. 67–83.
28. Bellah, Madsen, Sullivan, Swidler, and Tipton, *Habits of the Heart: Individualism and Commitment in American Life*, quote 285.
29. Robert Bellah, Richard Madsen, William M. Sullivan, Ann Swidler, and Steven M. Tipton, 1991, *The Good Society*, New York: Alfred A. Knopf.

30. James T. Kloppenberg, 2011, *Reading Obama: Dreams, Hopes, and the American Political Tradition*, Princeton, NJ: Princeton University Press, quote 265.
31. Barack Obama, "Why Organize? Problems and Promise in the Inner City," *Illinois Issues* (1988), republished 2008, http://illinoisissues.uis.edu.
32. Ibid.
33. Barack Obama, "Barack Obama Speaks out on Faith and Politics: 'Call to Renewal' Keynote Address," June 28, 2006, http://www.sojo.net; Barack Obama, 2006, *The Audacity of Hope: Thoughts on Reclaiming the American Dream*, New York: Three Rivers Press, pp. 195–226; see Kloppenberg, *Reading Obama: Dreams, Hopes, and the American Political Tradition*, 141–144.
34. Obama, "Barack Obama Speaks out on Faith and Politics: 'Call to Renewal' Keynote Address"; Robert Putnam, "Bowling Alone: America's Declining Social Capital," *Journal of Democracy* 6 (1995), pp. 65–78.
35. Obama, "Barack Obama Speaks out on Faith and Politics: 'Call to Renewal' Keynote Address."
36. Michael Falcone, Amy Walter, Z. Byron Wolf, "Arizona Shooting Touches Off Fierce Debate Over Political Rhetoric," ABC News: The Note, (January 9, 2011), http://blogs.abcnews.com, quotes; Peter Grier, "Jared Lee Loughner: What is Known About Tucson, Arizona Shooting Suspect," *Christian Science Monitor* (January 10, 2011).
37. The White House, Office of the Press Secretary, "Remarks by the President at a Memorial Service for the Victims of the Shooting in Tucson, Arizona," January 12, 2011, http://www.whitehouse.gov.
38. This section adapts material from Gary Dorrien, "Beyond State and Market: Christianity and the Future of Economic Democracy," *CrossCurrents* (Summer 1995), pp. 184–204.
39. See Michael J. Sandel, 1996, *Democracy's Discontent: America in Search of a Public Philosophy*, Cambridge: Harvard University Press, pp. 3–24; Arthur M. Schlesinger Jr., 1986, *The Cycles of American History*, Boston: Houghton Mifflin, pp. 23-49; Robert Dahl, 1985, *A Preface to Economic Democracy*, Berkeley: University of California Press; Howard Zinn, 1995, *A People's History of the United States, 1492-Present*, New York: HarperCollins; Gary Dorrien, 2009, *Economy, Difference, Empire: Social Ethics for Social Justice*, New York: Columbia University Press, pp. 143–144.
40. Barack Obama, "Remarks by the President in Sate of the Union Address," The White House, Office of the Press Secretary (January 27, 2010), http://www.whitehouse.gov.
41. Barack Obama, "State of the Union Address, 2011" (January 25, 2011), http://www.npr.org/2011/01/26.
42. Warren E. Buffett, "Stop Coddling the Super-Rich," *New York Times* (August 15, 2011).

CROSSCURRENTS
BOOK

Sexuality and the Jesus Tradition
William Loader, Grand Rapids: Eerdmans, 2005, pp. 288 + viii, pb, $30.00.

Enoch, Levi, and Jubilees on Sexuality, Attitudes Towards Sexuality in the Early Enoch Literature, The Aramaic Levi Document, and the Book of Jubilees
William Loader, Grand Rapids: Eerdmans, 2007, pp. 350 + viii, pb, $30.00.

The Pseudepigrapha on Sexuality, Attitudes toward Sexuality in Apocalyptic Testaments, Legends, Wisdom, and Related Literature
William Loader, Grand Rapids: Eerdmans, 2011, pp. 571 + xii, pb, $65.00.

William Loader is an Australian scholar and he likes sex. That is, he likes to write about it. He is prolific regarding the topic, having written three important volumes and some interesting articles on the subject. Moreover, he was gracious enough to review my book, *Sex in the Bible, A New Consideration* (Praeger, 2006) in the *Review of Biblical Literature*, for which I thank him and herewith return the favor. Loader is professor emeritus of NT at Murdoch University, Perth, Western Australia. He is busy with a five-volume series exploring attitudes toward sexuality in Judaism and Christianity during the Greco-Roman era. Eerdmans began to publish this series in 2005, and this review considers the three volumes that have already arrived.

Whereas my books on sex (CF also *The Spirituality of Sex*, Praeger 2009) are written in a pastoral and psychotherapeutic vein for popular consumption, Loader's volumes are works of consummate scholarship oriented toward the academic community. They are careful exegetical textual studies and designed to present the worldview and value system evidenced in those texts. Together they constitute a watershed mass of data and interpretation that will surely prevail as the standard works in this field of ancient cultures for the twenty-first century at least.

The first volume concerns sex in the Jesus tradition and has three parts: Sex and Danger: Passion and Responsibility, Order and Chaos: Marriage and Divorce, and Celibacy and Hope: Interim Choices. Each of these is a basket into which Loader has placed a series of chapters. The first section addresses small textual selections from Mt five, fifteen, and eighteen, and Mk seven and nine. After treating these key texts exegetically and hermeneutically, he develops his conclusions about sexual immorality manifested by the attitudes, actions, and assumptions present in those texts.

Section two carefully interprets Mt 5:31-2, and 19:9, Mk 10:11-12, Lu 16:18 and I Cor. 7:10-22 as the Sayings Texts and also treats the controversies in Mk 10:2-12 and Mt 19:3-12, finishing the section with an essay on John the Baptist and Herod Antipas. The final section is the largest and includes the Synoptic Gospels' Resurrection ideology related to sexuality, and various practical aspects of life under God's reign, such as the sexual issues of Eunuchs, celibacy, family, discipleship, virgins, widows, sacred people and things, and the like. He completes the book with an essay on the source of the notion of celibacy.

Loader's motivation to write these books on the perspectives on sexuality in Second Temple Judaism lies in the controversies about sexuality that arose within the Church during the last two decades, particularly about homosexual orientation and behavior. Loader notes that the history of the values concerning sexuality "is extraordinarily complex." He notes that "Approaching the issue of sexuality in the Jesus tradition is like looking out of the window of an aircraft and noting points on a landscape which emerge above the mist and fog that holds all else from view. There is so much we do not know..." (231). Nonetheless, it is a gratifying surprise to have the large panoply of concise insights that the author is able to derive from his careful exegesis of the few brief texts that the NT offers about the view of sexuality held by Jesus and the early church.

Loader's second sexuality volume addresses the Aramaic Levi Document, Early Enoch Literature, and the Book of Jubilees, all Jewish Second Temple literature. This volume is structured very similarly to the first one. There are three parts, each treating one of the documents listed in the title. Within each part the chapters critically analyze short selections of text from the document under consideration. In part one Loader analyzes material from the Book of the Watchers and The Book of Dream Visions from I Enoch, and such related material from that large document as the story of the birth of Noah. Part two contains a number of essays on special sexually oriented passages, such as the story of Levi and the Shechem Incident, women who desecrate the community, The Prayer of Levi, Isaac's instruction to Levi about marriage and sexual misbehavior, family life, and predictions of the future.

Part three is the largest part of this volume. It analyzes The Book of Jubilees, which scholars often consider a second writing of the Pentateuch without primary focus on the Torah or the revelation from Sinai. There are four chapters in this section of the book, which runs from page 113 to 285. It offers us (1) chapters on warnings about sexual misbehavior, a list of wrongdoing by the Watchers, Ham and Noah, Abraham, Sarai and Pharaoh, Circumcision, and the sin of Lot/destruction of Sodom; (2) chapters on the problems of Intermarriage and Rape: Dinah, Reuben and Bilhah, Joseph and Potiphar's wife, Noah and his progeny, Abraham and his progeny, Isaac and Jacob and their progeny, and an essay on the language of sexual misbehavior; and (3) chapters on such questions as creation and marriage, Abraham and Sarah, Rebecca and Isaac, and Jacob, Leah, and Rachel.

Loader makes the important point, in this second volume, that the ancient cultures and societies he addresses here would not have seen sexual behavior or misbehavior as such a major moral–ethical issue, as we do today in our rather puritanical western world. Their reason for raising the issue has mainly to do with the fact that ancient narratives regarding sexuality such as those in Genesis six and Genesis three are clues to how things unfolded in history and how the world and the human struggle is to be understood. The cautions and proscriptions regarding sexual behavior have mainly to do with keeping that unfolding history as non-turbulent as possible. One of the interesting aspects of Loader's analysis is his emphasis upon the difficulty of knowing just exactly what the sexual language means in these ancient documents, because the ethical perspective of those ancient cultures differed significantly from ours today.

Loader's third volume in this series, and the latest to appear, addresses the Pseudepigrapha, that is the attitudes on sexuality of the apocalypses, testaments, legends, wisdom literature, and related Second Temple Period documents. This volume includes a thirty-six-page contribution by Ibolya Balla on *Ben Sirach*. We are accustomed to Loader's structure and methodology by now, and predictably he has divided this volume into three parts: the first on the apocalypses, testaments, and related writings; the second on histories, legends, and related writings; and the final one on psalms, wisdom literature, and fragments.

Part one treats the Parables of Enoch (I Enoch 37-71), 2 Enoch, The Sibylline Oracles, and literature from Jeremiah, Baruch, 4 Ezra, 2 Baruch, and the testaments of Abraham, Moses, Job, and Solomon. Part two addresses the LXX and later works such as The Lives of the Prophets and Martyrdom of Isaiah, the Story of Zosimus, the Life of Adam and Eve, and the Apocalypse of Moses. Part three critiques the Psalms of Solomon, Ben Sirach, the Wisdom of Solomon, 4 Maccabees, Theodotus, Ezekiel the Tragedian, and other lesser known documents of ancient Jewish literature.

Loader's three volumes are massive studies of the literature he addresses; however, they are largely filled with the retelling of the narratives in the ancient documents as the basis for reflection and interpretation of their sexual statements or implications. He has labored hard and long to gather the material and organizing its presentation in readable and illuminating ways. It is not likely that scholars of Second Temple Judaism will find in these volumes anything that they did not already know. However, we are given two gifts from the author. First, Loader has assembled all of the material in Second Temple Literature that has any significant reference to human sexuality. Second, he has assembled the fairly wide spectrum of scholarly opinion regarding these texts. Readers who are not scholars of this ancient period or its documents will find in Loader's volumes an encyclopedic collection of illumining material, should they happen to develop the rare interest in this esoteric material in this academic form, and actually undertake the labor to read it.

Eerdmans has presented these three volumes exceedingly attractively, as usual, and the author and publisher have appropriately conspired to make these books accessible in detail. A cryptic summary for each chapter, ample indexes of modern and ancient authors, and ancient sources, plus a wonderfully rich bibliography finishes off each volume in a most professional manner. Harold Attridge of Yale observed that "Loader's ambitious project... is timely and potentially significant for contemporary debates about sexual morality. His vigorous historical approach provides an in-depth study of the primary sources, with attention to all of the concerns that they express about human sexual behavior and identity." This view is seconded by John J. Collins, and Kelley Coblentz Bautch. George J. Brooke avers that this work is "highly stimulating... intellectually, that is." Where will one find more graphic praise?

—*J. Harold Ellens*

Works Cited

Ellens, J. Harold (2006), *Sex in the Bible, A New Consideration*, Westport, CT: Praeger.

Ellens, Jay Harold (2009), *The Spirituality of Sex*, Westport, CT: Praeger.

CROSSCURRENTS BOOK

William Loader
Sexuality and the New Testament, Understanding Key Texts
Louisville, KY: Westminster John Knox, 2010. pp. 166 + viii, pb, npi.

William Loader is Professor Emeritus of NT Studies at Murdoch University, Perth, Australia. He has written numerous books on sexuality as it is described in the biblical and Second Temple Jewish documents. This present volume is the one dealing mostly with the books unique to the Christian scriptures. His works are well reviewed and widely known and used. Judith Lieu of Cambridge University declares, "Loader brings an honest and authoritative voice to the discussion of what the NT says about human sexuality. He invites his readers to join in a serious engagement with the scriptural texts in their social and historical context, and in so doing he leaves them with the challenge of wrestling with how those texts should be read today."

Sexuality in the New Testament is a neat little handbook of seven chapters, 126 pages, and forty pages of excellent end papers that include chapter notes, as well as indexes of ancient and biblical sources, modern authors, and subjects addressed in his text. He treats in-depth such issues as his chapter titles suggest: Engaging the far and the near: where to begin; "With a man as with a woman"; model marriage and the household; adultery, attitude, and disorder; divorce and remarriage; Has sex a future? the question of celibacy; and sex on the brain, love and hope.

Loader launches his address to this universally interesting, indeed intriguing, topic with the observation that we are all sexual and are the individual experts on our own sexuality; and understanding how the people of the Bible thought of sexuality will influence how we view it and respond to each other sexually. "Our sexual responses are about more than what we do with our genitalia; they encompass also our attitudes, thoughts, and fantasies..., sexuality engages us inside and out" (1).

This book is not about sexual ethics but about the NT, a world much different from ours, in that sex was considered sacred, intended for pregnancy, hence restricted to family life, and held overtones of concern for purity, loyalty, and exclusive commitment. Loader's second chapter is an extended and rather complete exposition of NT passages on homosexuality. Loader concludes that the Bible is against it. He fails to distinguish adequately whether the NT is addressing cultic homosexual behavior by heterosexuals or the daily life of homosexual couples. This results from his inadequately addressing whether the culture understood the distinction between homosexual behavior and inborn orientation to same-sex love. Most readers will find his chapter entirely persuasive in that it aligns with the traditional negative view of homosexuality and concludes that the NT does as well. He points out that it is interesting that Jesus does not comment on this issue, assuming that it just never came up. Only Paul significantly addresses significantly it in the NT.

Loader is quite sure that the NT stands for no sex until betrothal, universal monogamy, sex for procreation, sex for the joy of it in the marriage union, refraining from adultery, forgiveness of adultery for the preservation of the marriage union, and avoidance of divorce. He devotes his fifth chapter to a rather scholastic exposition of the incredibly enigmatic NT observations about divorce and remarriage, passages that in the end are impossible to sort out coherently. His concluding paragraph on this matter is as enigmatic as the NT passages, "Thus despite the relative strength of evidence about divorce and remarriage in the NT, and its consistency in depicting marriage as indissoluble (except where broken by adultery), we are left with many historical questions about how these prohibitions worked themselves out, not to speak of the way they were understood and applied to divers situations" (97).

On celibacy, Loader asserts that Paul is for it as a special vocation of those devoted to kingdom work. However, the author fails to distinguish adequately between the early Pauline letters and the Deutero-Pauline epistles, and fails to indicate the shift in that literature regarding celibacy, associated with the eschatological shift from the notion of immediately impending parousia and the delayed parousia as it applies to the matter of Pauline emphasis upon celibacy. Most folks have noticed that in his early letters Paul suggests that since Jesus' return on the clouds of heaven is imminent, establishing a marriage and family is hardly worth the trouble or appropriate. In the later Pauline literature, the disposition has shifted and we have guidance on how marriage should be established and managed, because "we are obviously in it for the long run" because Jesus' promise to return in the first generation did not prove true and real.

This neat and highly readable little volume will strike a welcome note with most traditional believers for two reasons. First, it essentially reinforces the historic posture on sex championed by the church since the fourth century after Christ, despite the very different Christian perspective on human sexuality of such early Christian leaders as Epiphanes and the early Christian Stoics. Second, "most who as believers encounter those [NT] texts do so with a certain confidence that there is something permanent which addresses us ... and which offers guidance and hope as we live with our sexuality" (125). The positive side of Loader's exposition will be seen in its reinforcement of the general conservative Christian posture on sex. The negative aspect lies in the fact that it does not provide a fresh view of the NT that would afford more openness and freedom from the sexual rigidity, anxiety, constraint, and shame that the sexual tone of historic Christianity has induced. For a more nuanced explication of the sexual passages of the OT and NT, the reader may wish to compare Loader's work with my *Sex in the Bible, A New Consideration* (Praeger 2006), to which Loader refers in his exposition.

Nonetheless, the notable David Instone-Brewer, Senior Research Fellow in Rabbinics and the NT at the University of Cambridge, has this compliment for Loader's present work. Loader has brought together sources from the ancient world and opinions from a wide range of scholarship in many contentious areas concerning sexuality, homosexuality, divorce, submission of women, sex outside marriage, and celibacy. In all of these, he avoids leading the witness, letting the texts speak for themselves. He states the opinion of other scholars and occasionally of himself, but his aim is to educate and not preach.

—*J. Harold Ellens*

CONTRIBUTORS

Rachel Barenblat holds an MFA from the Bennington Writing Seminars and is author of *70 faces*, a collection of Torah poems (Phoenicia Publishing, 2011). She serves a small congregation in western Massachusetts and blogs as The Velveteen Rabbi.

Eric Caplan is the chair of the Department of Jewish Studies, McGill University. He is the vice president of the Mordecai M. Kaplan Center for Jewish Peoplehood and the author of *From Ideology to Liturgy: Reconstructionist Worship and American Liberal Judaism* (Hebrew Union College Press, 2002).

Gary Dorrien is the Reinhold Niebuhr Professor of Social Ethics at Union Theological Seminary and Professor of Religion at Columbia University. His thirteen books include the trilogy *The Making of American Liberal Theology*.

J. Harold Ellens is a Professor of Philosophy and Psychology Emeritus, Presbyterian Theologian and Pastor Emeritus, Research Scholar in Second Temple Judaism and Christian Origins at University of Michigan Department of Near Eastern Studies, Psychotherapist in Private Practice, and retired US Army Colonel. He has authored, edited, or provided chapters for 167 published volumes and has written 165 professional journal articles. He is a noted international lecturer and has just returned from a lecture tour in the Far East and South Pacific, celebrating his 76th birthday twice, once in Inchon, Korea, and once in New York (having crossed the dateline overnight by way of the polar route).

Edward Feld is the senior editor of Mahzor Lev Shalem (Conservative) and author of *Spirit of Renewal: Faith After the Holocaust* (Jewish Lights) and *The Book of Revolutions: The Bible and the Formation of Judaism* (Aviv Press, forthcoming). He has served as Rabbi-in-Residence at the Jewish Theological Seminary of America, Rabbi of the Society for the Advancement of Judaism, and Hillel Director of Princeton University. He is Director of the Rabbinic Companionship Program, counseling and coaching rabbis in the field, and former Educational Director of Rabbis for Human Rights—North America.

Leah Hochman directs the Louchheim School for Judaic Studies at the University of Southern California and is assistant professor of Jewish Thought at Hebrew Union College-Jewish Institute of Religion in Los Angeles. She received her B.A. from Pitzer College and her M.A./Ph.D. in religion and literature from Boston University; she is currently finishing a book project on conceptions of ugliness in 18th century thought.

Catherine Madsen is the author of *The Bones Reassemble: Reconstituting Liturgical Speech*; *In Medias Res: Liturgy for the*

Estranged; and a novel, *A Portable Egypt*. She is Bibliographer at the Yiddish Book Center in Amherst, MA.

Gabriel Moran is a professor in the department of Humanities and the Social Sciences, New York University. He was director of the doctoral program in religious education and teaches courses in the philosophy and the history of education. He has also taught at Manhattan College, New York Theological Seminary, Boston College and special courses at two dozen other universities.

Vanessa L. Ochs is a professor in Religious Studies and Jewish Studies at the University of Virginia. She is the author, most recently, of *Inventing Jewish Ritual* (JPS), winner of a National Jewish Book Award, and is writing a "biography" of the Passover Haggadah for Princeton University Press.

James W. Perkinson is a long-time activist and educator from inner-city Detroit, currently teaching as Professor of Social Ethics at the Ecumenical Theological Seminary and lecturing in Intercultural Communication Studies at the Oakland University (Michigan). He holds a Ph.D. in theology from the University of Chicago, is the author of *White Theology: Outing Supremacy in Modernity* and *Shamanism, Racism, and Hip–Hop Culture: Essays on White Supremacy and Black Subversion*, has written extensively in both academic and popular journals on questions of race, class, and colonialism in connection with religion and urban culture, and is a recognized artist on the spoken-word poetry scene in the inner city.

Caroline Rody is Professor of English at the University of Virginia, where she teaches courses on contemporary Jewish fiction and on a range of subjects in ethnic American and women's fiction. Her books are *The Interethnic Imagination: Roots and Passages in Contemporary Asian American Fiction* (Oxford UP, 2009) and *The Daughter's Return: African-American and Caribbean Women's Fictions of History* (Oxford UP, 2001).

Eric Murphy Selinger is Associate Professor of English at DePaul University, where he teaches courses on poetry and popular fiction. His books include *Jewish American Poetry: Poems, Commentary, and Reflections* (UPNE/Brandeis UP, 2000) and *Ronald Johnson: Life and Works* (NPF, 2008); he is a frequent contributor to *Parnassus: Poetry in Review*.

www.ingramcontent.com/pod-product-compliance
Lightning Source LLC
Chambersburg PA
CBHW040259170426
43193CB00020B/2947